> Then weave for us a garment of brightness;
> May the warp be the white lights of morning,
> May the weft be the red light of evening,
> May the fringes be the falling rain,
> May the border be the standing rainbow.
>
> *Excerpted from a Tewa Song*

Navajo Moki-Style Blanket (*beeldléí* or *nakhai bich'ídei*), 1885–1900

210.8 x 154.3 cm

Donor: Martha A. Jenks; 652.G.122

Remarks: This blanket design is featured in the Hubbell Trading Post "rug study" and is illustrated in a 1905 oil painting by artist Bertha Little. These paintings were commissioned by Juan Lorenzo Hubbell to serve as templates of older patterns for Navajo weavers to copy. Such textiles have come to be known as Hubbell Revivals.

Analysis: The textile is a plain, weft-faced tapestry weave with lazy lines. It is woven of three-ply, s-spun, S-twist machine-spun yarns and four-ply, z-spun, S-twist machine-spun woolen yarns. The dyes are aniline.

COMMON THREADS
Pueblo and Navajo Textiles in the Southwest Museum

Kathleen Whitaker

With analysis assistance by Susie Hart

Southwest Museum
Los Angeles

Dedicated to the Memory of Norman F. Sprague, Jr.

Common Threads: Pueblo and Navajo Textiles in the Southwest Museum is published in conjunction with an exhibition of the same title organized by the Southwest Museum, Los Angeles, and presented at the Southwest Museum at LACMA West, October 25, 1998, to September 26, 1999.

This publication is made possible by The National Endowment for the Arts, The Norman F. Sprague, Jr. Foundation, and the Mildred E. and Harvey S. Mudd Foundation.

The exhibition is made possible by The Getty Grant Program for Interpretive Projects, The Ralph M. Parsons Foundation, The James Irvine Foundation, The Weingart Foundation, The Rockefeller Foundation, and the Camilla Chandler Family Foundation.

Published by the Southwest Museum, 234 Museum Drive, P.O. Box 41558, Los Angeles, California 90041-0558.

© 1998 by the Southwest Museum. All rights reserved. No part of this publication may be reproduced in any manner without written permission of the publisher.

ISBN: 0-916561-72-0

Edited by Karen Jacobson
Produced for the Southwest Museum by
Legacy Communications, Inc., Santa Barbara, California
Designed by Roger L. Morrison
Printed in Singapore

Maps by Bernie Granados Jr.
Illustrations by Jack McCord

Photography Credits
All photographs by Schenck & Schenck Photography, except for the following:
The Braun Research Library: endsheets and pp. 16, 17, 18, 21, 25, 28, 33, 55, 56, 58, 59, 65
The Nebraska State Historical Society: p. 34
Larry Reynolds: back flap
Rani Tagland: p. 33

Cover:
Detail of **Navajo Transitional Blanket-Rug** (*beeldléí*), 1885–1902 [p. 48]

Front flap:
Navajo Woman's Manta (*beeldléí or biil*), 1875–1900
94 x 110.5 cm
Donor: Mrs. Edward Lawrence Doheny; 761.G.1
Remarks: The donor purchased this textile in Albuquerque, New Mexico, in 1917.
Analysis: This is a float, uneven (2/1), and diamond twill tapestry weave with lazy lines. The border diamond twill is unusual in that, through the manipulation of the float weave technique, the pattern merges into a checkerboard. It is woven of one-ply, z-spun native handspun wool; four-ply, z-spun, S-twist machine-spun yarn; and three- and four-ply, s-spun (sxs) raveled American flannel wool. The orange/white diagonal twill in the central body of the manta has bits of American flannel carded with native handspun wool. The warp is four-ply, z-spun, S-twist machine-spun cotton twine. Aniline dyes that have faded and shifted in color define the pattern.

Inside front cover:
Acoma Pueblo Governor Eusebius and his staff in front of the old church, dressed in men's shoulder blankets. The governor wears a commercially manufactured blanket, while the others appear to be wearing blankets of either Pueblo or Navajo manufacture.
Photograph by George Wharton James, 1897.

Inside back cover:
The Shiprock Tribal Fair in Shiprock, New Mexico, 1914. This annual event was started in 1909 by Superintendent William T. Shelton, Indian agent to the Navajos. Its purpose was to benefit them by enabling the Indian traders to exhibit and sell their finest crafts and by encouraging skills in animal husbandry and agriculture. The fair was held during late October, and the finest blankets and rugs were generally made available for sale. *Photographer unknown.*

Opposite:
Hopi Loom Sampler with Angak Katcina Figure, 1929
80 x 58.5 cm
Donor: General Charles McCormack Reeve Fund; 491.G.230A
Remarks: Southwest Museum curator Mark Raymond Harrington collected this sampler from the Hopi village of Oraibi, Arizona, in 1929.
Analysis: This is a plain, weft-faced tapestry weave. It is woven of one-ply, z-spun native handspun wool and four-ply (X3), z-spun, S-twist machine-spun yellow woolen yarn used three strands at a time. Aniline-dyed yarns and yarns spun from the natural colors of the wool define the pattern.

CONTENTS

Foreword	*7*
Preface	*9*
The Legacy of Spider Woman	*10*
Pueblo and Navajo Textiles	*13*
In Search of a Weaving Aesthetic *The Impact of Cultural Interaction on Pueblo and Navajo Textiles*	*49*
Glossary	*67*
References	*70*
Acknowledgments	*71*

Navajo Pictorial Rug (*beeldléí*), 1925–32

138 x 87 cm

Donor: Fred Kimpton Hinchman; 535.G.587

Remarks: With pictorial elements of two katcinas, this rug was originally identified as Hopi-made by the donor, probably due to its subject matter. Alfred Whiting (1976: 413) notes that a few Hopi male weavers made limited attempts to copy the Navajo manufactures. He wrote: "Thus, we find 'Navajo' style blankets with borders, broken band designs, and even lazy lines woven by Hopi men." The fineness of this rug's weave and technology, however, seems to suggest a Navajo origin. Moreover, Navajo weavers living near Flagstaff, Arizona, were incorporating Hopi patterns into their rugs and tapestries to meet the demand of the burgeoning tourist trade during the 1930s.

Analysis: This is a plain, weft-faced weave with lazy lines. It is woven of one-ply, z-spun native handspun wool. Indigo blue and aniline-dyed yarns and yarns spun of the natural colors of the wool define the design.

FOREWORD

The opening of the exhibition *Common Threads: Pueblo and Navajo Textiles in the Southwest Museum* celebrates the vitality of the oldest museum in the City of Los Angeles. Our collaboration with the Los Angeles County Museum of Art to develop exhibition space in the newly renovated LACMA West building opens a new chapter in the history of the Southwest Museum. Although we are mindful of the Southwest Museum's role in preserving the past, our vision is fixed firmly on the future. Our mission is to enhance the public understanding and appreciation of the peoples and the cultures represented in the museum's collections.

The textile collection of the Southwest Museum, featured in this exhibition, is generally considered to be one of the finest of its kind in the world. In the 1990s a number of funding agencies and individuals recognized the importance of this rare collection and its value to future generations. Grants to research, conserve, and document the collection have been generously provided by the National Endowment for the Arts, the Institute of Museum and Library Services, the Ahmanson Foundation, and an individual benefactor, Ms. Anna Moore. The support and vision of these agencies and individuals over the past decade have made it possible for Chief Curator Kathleen Whitaker and the museum's staff to conduct the valuable research necessary to achieve a greater understanding of the collection and make it available to the community.

It is especially heartening that other museums and funding agencies have recognized the importance of this collection and the potential of this exhibition. The board and staff of the Los Angeles County Museum of Art were gracious enough to invite us to share a gallery at LACMA West, recognizing that the Southwest Museum's collections enhance and complement LACMA's encyclopedic holdings. To support this opportunity to make the Southwest Museum's exhibits and programs available to a much broader audience, numerous individuals and several funding agencies have contributed more than $1 million over the past year.

The National Endowment for the Arts funded research, documentation of the collection, and a portion of the cost of this catalogue. The Mildred E. and Harvey S. Mudd Foundation and the Norman F. Sprague Jr. Foundation provided funds to cover the costs of publications associated with this and future exhibitions. The Getty Grant Program, the Ralph M. Parsons Foundation, the Weingart Foundation, the James Irvine Foundation, and the Rockefeller Foundation have generously supported the gallery construction and the planning, design, fabrication, and installation of the exhibition. Camilla Chandler Frost made a substantial personal commitment, as did a number of present and past members of the Southwest Museum's Board of Trustees.

We are very grateful to all those who have, through their gifts and hard work, contributed to this effort to make this important collection a part of the thriving arts community in Los Angeles.

Duane H. King
Executive Director
Southwest Museum

Navajo Large Tapestry (*beeldléí*), 1900–1917

346.7 x 344.2 cm

Donor: Mrs. Edward Laurence Doheny; 761.G.32

Remarks: This textile was purchased in Albuquerque, New Mexico, in 1917 by the Doheny family.

Analysis: This is a very fine plain, weft-faced tapestry weave with lazy lines. It is woven of all four-ply, z-spun, S-twist machine-spun yarns. The dyes are aniline.

PREFACE

This work, together with the exhibition it accompanies, explores the aesthetic nature of Pueblo and Navajo textiles as an expression of the weaver's perceptions and culture. It is based upon the comprehensive holdings of the Southwest Museum, Los Angeles, which, among its more than 2,123 Southwestern textiles, has 1,764 Pueblo and Navajo examples, dating from c. A.D. 1275 to the present. More than 78 percent of these were manufactured between c. 1800 and 1940.

The museum's evolving collection serves as a remarkable testament to the creative vitality and productive energy of the Pueblo and Navajo weavers, and each textile is inextricably linked to their experiences, their beliefs, and their roles as individuals within a culture. The fundamental nature of weaving is such that it serves as a remarkably accurate window through which one can view Navajo and Pueblo life. The passion, creativity, and innovation revealed in each fabric tell us something about the often unknown weavers who put thought, sometimes humor, and always an aesthetic and spiritual quality into each piece.

Over the years textiles from both groups have been brilliantly adaptive, as their makers responded to often-disruptive historical events. Yet the alterations in the appearance of the textiles should never be confused with assimilation but should instead be viewed in light of the common threads of cultural and artistic continuity within each group. Navajo and Pueblo weavers look at their work as having communal as well as individual significance, so each example should be seen as a collaborative model of cooperation and sharing. Most importantly, in weaving, the process of creating overrides the cultural importance of the object created. The import of this study, then, lies in the overarching theme that these textiles have a value that goes beyond simple artistic expression. In both cultures the weaving art form embodies a dynamic, kinetic force, fostering a connection to the past as well as a sense of hope for the future—always changing but always reflecting the cultural source from which it emanates.

This catalogue presents a selection of 68 Pueblo and Navajo textiles that demonstrate the continuity and change within these cultures, illustrating a progression of styles and periods of manufacture. Moreover, the pieces articulate, in numbers and in kind, not only the monumental efforts of the artists but also, secondarily, the activities and tastes of the collectors who tried to preserve native art traditions by placing many of the materials they gathered in museums.

This catalogue is conceived as a companion volume to a major work currently in preparation, *Pueblo and Navajo Textiles in the Southwest Museum,* scheduled for publication in 1999. This second volume is divided into three sections. The first explores the history and collecting patterns of individuals who contributed Navajo and Pueblo textiles to the Southwest Museum from 1917 to 1998, highlighting five key early donors. It also includes a complete list of the donors, many of whom were ethnographers, photographers, writers, adventurers, and aficionados whose varied interests in the Indian "curio" created one of the finest collections of Navajo and Pueblo textiles in the world. Many of the early collectors were products of the Victorian age, and some were prominent members of Los Angeles society. By the very nature of their diverse interests and backgrounds, all were social "curiosities" themselves. The second section provides a comprehensive analysis of 270 textiles, illustrated in color, including information on fibers, dyes, and weave structure. Relevant archival and ethnographic information and study notes are also included. The third section offers an inclusive inventory of the museum's Navajo and Pueblo textile collection, complete with cultural classifications, dates of manufacture, accession numbers, and accompanying collection remarks.

Taken together, these publications represent a major contribution to the study of Pueblo and Navajo textiles, not least because they make the Southwest Museum's extraordinary collection of this material available to a much wider audience.

K.W.

THE LEGACY OF SPIDER WOMAN

According to stories of the Navajo and Pueblo, Spider Woman gave them knowledge of weaving and, in so doing, the ability to create beauty and the gifts of life on their looms. Both the craft and art of loom-woven creations have been perceived through, and perhaps motivated by, language, family relationships, and religious beliefs. Through these cultural traits Navajos and Pueblos share a common tradition, one that is sanctioned by a culture hero who taught them how to create with beauty, patience, understanding, and harmony. As a result, throughout its evolution weaving has been both a collective and an individual reinforcement of culture.

Weavers believe that the integrity and balance of a textile is observed in its wholeness. As a completed creation, a woven fabric embodies a design that is made up of isolated elements that are brought together in a single image. It absorbs the free-flowing energy of the culture from which it emanates, and it reflects the character of the individual weaver as an innovator and the role of the community as the weaver's connection to the spiritual and material worlds. Moreover, the textile is a product of individual action and creativity, it is adaptable in its use, and it embodies—through its fibers, dyes, and design—the processes of continuity and change that are essential features of culture. As such, weaving, in both action and purpose, might be regarded as a model for a Pueblo or Navajo approach to life and, therefore, requires the sanction of the deities to validate it.

Through the spiritual foundation of weaving, men and women of both cultures beautify their world and experience the good in it, and their art is integrated into the "web of life." They weave for family, for friends, for the good of the community, and always for the good they find within when they fulfill these responsibilities. Weaving can be an embodiment of the normal patterns of nature, and weavers know that when they are creating, they cannot be separated from goodness, health, happiness, and those qualities that help to balance life. It is the creation of beauty and the incorporation of oneself into this realm that represent the weaver's highest attainment. When working, weavers will discuss how the yarns and fibers guide and control the pattern, seeking their own path through the loom "web" until the textile is complete. The designs, they say, "come from the mind" and, as such, provide a link between the ancient past, the present, and the future.

The fundamental, and often unvoiced, thought of weavers is that Spider Woman is teaching, guiding, and ultimately directing their creation. When "it is finished in beauty," as the Navajo say, the textile becomes an expression of both the culture and the individual weaver in a special way—always controlled and balanced but also dynamic. The weaver—like the batten, the comb, and the loom frame itself—is merely another instrument, representing all that has been learned and all that remains to be learned.

While Spider Woman is the originator of weaving and spinning, she can be many other things in the stories of the people. In their belief systems the Navajo and Pueblo cultures have a number of helpers who assist their deities and man. These are beings who bridge the supernatural distance between man and the gods and who play major roles in cultural instruction. These cultural helpers fall into several categories and include almost all of the animals, even insects. Particularly notable among the insects are Spider Woman and Spider Man.

Among the Navajo, Spider Woman is often referred to as the "chief medicine woman" who gave the Twin Gods feathers to represent the thread of life and save them from peril, but they also recognize that she can be dangerous. Therefore, the Navajo counsel moderation in all things, even weaving. According to Navajo stories, when Spider Woman is angered, she sometimes has to be subdued with prayer and offerings of woven fabrics. Navajo Spider Woman tales also portray her as the wealthiest of the Pueblo people. This belief provides another link between the Pueblo and Navajo.

To the Hopi (a Pueblo group) she is a culture hero of the earth and its creatures, and cocreator with Tawa, the Sun God. She is often portrayed as the all-wise, all-knowing, all-powerful guardian of the Hopi people and grandmother to the Twins, the Little War Gods. To both the Pueblo and the Navajo she is also a symbol of the textile arts. Father Berard Haile (Franciscan Fathers 1910, 222) records the best known of the Navajo Spider Woman and Spider Man tales—an origin story that by its very nature appears to have been borrowed from the Pueblo.

> *The Spider Man drew some cotton from his side and instructed the Navaho to make a loom. The cotton-warp was made of Spider-web. The upper cross-pole was called sky or upper cord, the lower cross pole, earth or lower cord. The warp-sticks were made of sun rays, the upper strings, fastening the warp to the pole, of lightning, the lower strings of sun halo, the heald was a rock crystal, the cord-heald stick was made of sheet lightning and was secured to the warp strand by means of rain ray cords.*
>
> *The batten stick was also made of sun halo, while the comb was of white shell. Four spindles or distaffs were added to this, the disks of which were of cannel-coal, turquoise, abalone and white bead respectively, and the spindle-sticks of zig-zag lightning, flash lightning, and rain ray, respectively.*

Navajo Weaving Song

I weave in harmony.
  With the Earth I weave.
The strings are like rain,
  The rain touches my fingers.
There is beauty in my blanket.
  There is beauty all around me.
There is beauty above me.
  There is beauty below me
The plants speak to me,
  Mother Earth colors my rug.
I weave in harmony.

Navajo Woman's Manta (*beeldléí or biil*), 1890–1900

101.6 x 139.7 cm

Donor: Mrs. Edward Laurence Doheny; 761.G.2

Remarks: This manta incorporates "Spider Woman" crosses as the primary design motifs. It is identical to textiles woven at Hubbell's trading post c. 1885–1900. It was purchased by the Doheny family in Albuquerque, New Mexico, in 1917.

Analysis: This is a plain, weft-faced tapestry weave with lazy lines. It is woven of one-ply, z-spun native handspun wool. It has a gray and white one-ply, z-spun native handspun wool warp. Indigo- and aniline-dyed yarns and yarns spun from the natural brown color of the wool define the design.

Hopi Banded Blanket (*Pösaala*), 1870–80

176 x 113 cm

Donor: Fred Kimpton Hinchman; 535.G.515

Remarks: This is an unusual blanket design of Hopi manufacture. The donor purchased it from J. F. Snively, a Pasadena, California, art dealer who was in business during the 1920s and 1930s. The design and colors were highly influenced by the Spanish-Mexican Saltillo sarape.

Analysis: This is a plain, weft-faced weave with no lazy lines. It is woven of one-ply, z-spun native handspun merino wool; three-ply, s-spun (sxs) raveled worsted wool from cloth; three-ply, s-spun, S-twist machine-spun woolen yarn; and four-ply, z-spun, S-twist machine-spun worsted wool yarn. It is small. The brown warp is one-ply, z-spun native handspun merino wool. Indigo-, cochineal(?)-, vegetal(?)- (for the yellow-gold), and aniline-dyed yarns and yarns spun from the natural colors of the wool define the pattern. Some of the colors are completely fugitive.

Pueblo & Navajo Textiles

The Southwest Museum's collection of Pueblo and Navajo textiles incorporates some of the finest woven fabrics ever manufactured for use, trade, and commerce by indigenous Southwestern Indians. The growth of the museum's collection over a period of seventy-nine years is represented by these examples, beginning with the first donation, in 1917. Since that time more than 128 donors have given blankets, rugs, mantas, and other textiles to the museum. These works are the enduring legacy of Pueblo and Navajo weavers, past and present, who have resided in northeastern Arizona, central and northern New Mexico, and the southern reaches of Utah.

Pueblo representation in the museum's collection includes textiles made or collected in the Hopi villages of Oraibi, Hotevilla, Mishongnovi, and Shungopovi, in Arizona. The New Mexico pueblos include Zuni, Acoma, Santa Clara, Isleta, Santo Domingo, San Juan, and Jemez. Dates of manufacture for these textiles range from c. 1850 to 1979. Navajo textiles come from throughout the Southwest, which the Navajo called *Dinetah* (Navajo country), and date from c. 1800 to 1980. Selected examples of textiles manufactured during the Classic, Late Classic, and Transitional periods are featured, as well as twentieth-century textiles from representative reservation areas such as Chinle, Lukachukai, Kayenta, Ganado, Wide Ruins, Pine Springs, Shiprock, Fruitland, Farmington, Klagetoh, Toadlena, Two Gray Hills, Crystal, and Teec Nos Pos. This catalogue focuses primarily on textiles woven on upright looms with heddles.

Overall the collection spans a time period of approximately 180 years. During this period Pueblo and Navajo people became unwilling participants in American expansion into their territories, experiencing the devastating effects of disease and the ravages of warfare. They also became the beneficiaries of extensive trade; suffered the psychological impact of exile and confinement; tolerated the nation's drive, motivated by guilt and curiosity, to preserve things made by the "vanishing" American Indian; and endured the invasive effects of tourism after the completion of the transcontinental railroad. These circumstances shaped the social and political environments in which they lived and established the conditions under which most of the tapestries illustrated in this catalogue were created.

An Ethnohistorical Overview of Navajo and Pueblo Weaving

Although Pueblo and Navajo textiles evolved along different paths, reflecting the differences in the two cultures, they also shared common threads in the historical and individual experiences that shaped their development. Pueblo and Navajo weavers have been in contact for more than three centuries. In the eighteenth and early nineteenth centuries not only did their weaving styles and technology mirror each other, but both cultures also shared a rich complex of religious doctrines, social networks, and subsistence activities. They learned from each other, and each influenced the other in the choice of looms, materials, dyes, weaves, and designs. In fact, if it were not for certain technological variations in their weaving styles, which evolved over time, it would be difficult, if not impossible, to distinguish their fabrics. The loom technology

Hopi(?) or Navajo(?) Moki-Style Blanket
(*pösaala* [H] or *beeldléí* or *nakhai bich'idei* [N]),
1868–78

170.2 x 125 cm

Donor: C. B. Scoville Jr.; 518.G.15

Remarks: The difficulty in establishing a cultural origin for this textile lies in the technology. The textile has specific features that identify it with both Hopi and Navajo origins. On the one hand, it has no lazy lines (a Pueblo trait), it is fairly small, and the zigzag and chevron motifs as filler elements within the banded pattern seem to follow a general Pueblo orientation. On the other hand, the corners have embellished tassels, in keeping with a typical Navajo finish. There are weft picks of raveled cloth scattered throughout the weave.

Analysis: This is a plain, weft-faced tapestry weave. It is woven of one-ply, z-spun native handspun merino wool and four-ply, s-spun (sxs) raveled cloth. The dyes are indigo and cochineal, and the spun brown yarn is the natural color of the wool. The white wool has no dye.

used to create these fabrics has seen very little variation to the present day.

Early on, indigenous cotton and other plant fibers became the loom materials of choice for Pueblo weavers. Cotton was introduced to the Southwest from pre-Spanish Mexico, and while Kent (1957, 467) believes this may have been before the time of Christ, there is certain evidence of its existence before A.D. 700. It continued to be the Pueblos' preferred material for ceremonial garments for many centuries.

Along with the importation of cotton into the Southwest came the belt or backstrap loom from Mexico and Guatemala. By A.D. 800 the Pueblos were using a vertical loom whose upper bars were lashed to the roof beams of a Pueblo home or *kiva* (a subterranean ceremonial chamber). This apparatus is still in use today. This loom was later adopted by Navajo weavers. The cotton and (after 1539) wool materials were prepared for weaving by spinning or twisting the fibers on a hand-manipulated spindle whorl. This type of shaft-and-whorl spinning was associated with all materials prepared by Pueblo and Navajo weavers.

In 1539, when contact was made with the outside world, new cultural traits, domesticated animals, and other factors promoted innovation in the indigenous Southwest weaving industry. The Spanish, for example, introduced a new sheep-raising economy and made European manufactured goods more accessible. Thereafter, both Pueblo- and Navajo-woven fabrics enjoyed an increase in demand and production, incorporating raveled and prespun (machine-spun) materials, the use of aniline dyes, and greater flexibility in weave structures, design, and style. Clothing styles also changed. American expansion into the Southwest and the importation of European- and American-produced goods led to more obvious, material changes in Pueblo and Navajo fabrics. Yet over the decades, despite these changes, weavers continued to be guided by their own individual cultural requirements. Thus, the appearance and use of Pueblo and Navajo fabrics took decidedly different paths in their development.

Bernie Granados Jr.

A Brief History of Pueblo Textiles

The Pueblo manufacture of woven textiles and the decoration of such fabrics are traditions that reach into a two-thousand-year history. Through the centuries these techniques have undergone few changes and so provide a link to the ancient past. Early in their history Pueblo weavers and their woven goods responded to a different set of cultural and behavioral priorities than those that have guided their Navajo neighbors.

Pueblo weavers belonged to a community whose means of subsistence was primarily horticultural. Their creativity was connected to a communal thought process and dictated by rigid cultural controls, social rites of passage, class status, ritual, and technical proficiency. Woven garments were made for individuals who had special family and clan relationships to the weaver. Such articles of clothing also identified the wearer's age and gender, marked initiations into social groups, and signaled one's social standing. In addition, it was believed that the attire in which one was buried indicated his or her social standing to the inhabitants of the Underworld (Wright 1979, 11). Moreover, styles of clothing testified to a sedentary way of life. Among the Hopi, men were the weavers. Among the New Mexico Pueblos, weavers could be either male or female. Because Pueblo textiles conform to a type of social formula, this dynamic art form should be appreciated for its cultural authenticity and technical proficiency, rather than for its variety and innovation.

Cotton, the preferred material of the early weavers, enjoyed symbolic importance. It was associated

Three young Hopi girls in 1901 from the village of Oraibi, wearing *kanelkwasas*, or blanket-dresses. These were worn either as dresses or as capes over the dresses, as seen in this photo. Much of the literature refers to this style of clothing as a manta, which is the Spanish word for blanket. Note the man's shoulder blanket, or *pösaala*, draped over the wall behind them.
Photograph by George Wharton James.

Hopi Black Wool Manta-Dress with Diamond Twill Borders (*kanelkwasa*), 1925–37

73 x 46 cm

Donor: Fred Kimpton Hinchman; 535.G.726

Remarks: A fine example of a small child's dress with attached red shoulder straps and red and green embellishments. The donor purchased this in 1937.

Analysis: This is a float, even (2/2), and diamond twill (outer borders) weave. Alongside the inner border is an uneven twill of "hills and vales," consisting of alternating sections of 2/1 and 1/2 weave structures. The fabric is woven of one-ply, z-spun native handspun wool. It is sewn together with four-ply, z-spun, S-twist machine-spun woolen yarns. The dyes are indigo and aniline red and green.

A Zuni woman in her finest clothing, 1879. Her blanket-dress, or *Bi:sale'*, was probably of dark brown-black wool. It is a float diagonal twill weave with borders embroidered in indigo blue, typical of the period between 1870 and 1880. The negative line design at the border of the dress appears to be that of the swallowtail butterfly with the Spanish-influenced fleur-de-lis. Over this she wears a Hopi blue-and-red-bordered white cotton manta (*atö 'ö*, peeking out on the left), probably traded from the Hopi, and the outer garment is also a *Bi:sale'*, worn as a shoulder blanket or shawl.
Photograph by John K. Hillers.

Zuni Embroidered Brown Wool Manta-Dress (*E:hay Yadonanna*), 1870–90

105 x 140 cm

Donor: Fred Kimpton Hinchman; 535.G.608

Remarks: Early Zuni-style mantas had borders that were most often embroidered with indigo blue–dyed native handspun yarns, although occasionally some dresses incorporated red embroidery patterns. This dress carries the Spanish-derived fleur-de-lis motif along the inner edge of the design border. Also incorporated in this pattern is the swallowtail butterfly, a woman's symbol and a symbol of beauty. This example also displays the yarn ring tassels at the corners of the dress.

Analysis: This is a plain, balanced weave on the borders (covered by the embroidery), with a float, even (2/2) diagonal twill weave in the main body of the dress. It is woven of one-ply, z-spun native handspun wool. The embroidery is of one-ply, z-spun native handspun indigo blue–dyed wool. Embroidery techniques include the outline, overcast, whip, and herringbone stitches.

with light clouds as well as with *katcina* messengers (ancestral spirit helpers) and the rain that was so critical to most of the Pueblos, who practiced dry farming. Cotton was grown in the Hopi villages in Arizona and in New Mexico, probably as far north as San Juan Pueblo, and at Acoma and Isleta, but little, if any, was raised at Zuni. From all accounts the Hopi were the main suppliers to all the Pueblos.

The arrival of the Spanish in the Southwest changed the style and type of Pueblo textiles. The cultivation and use of cotton soon declined and was gradually replaced by wool provided by churro sheep, a Spanish import. This wool was a soft, long, lustrous fiber with little grease or crimp and was easy to work by hand. By 1870 merino sheep had replaced the churro. This breed produced a short, curly, and greasy wool that was difficult to process by hand. Commercial cotton twine had also begun to replace handspun cotton by this time and was frequently used as warps in wide-loom fabrics.

Principal among the Pueblo manufactures was the small rectangular textile referred to as a manta. There are six styles of manta. All are wider than they are long; that is, the length of the warps (or the foundation of the weave structure) is shorter than the width of the fabric. Mantas were commonly woven in striped or figured-twill weave or in plain-weave structures that have no embellishment. They were generally woven of natural fibers. Occasionally they were dyed, and some fabrics were embellished by plaiting, brocading, or embroidery.

As a rule mantas were woven of either white cotton or natural brown or black wool, although some were cut from U.S. Army blankets. The six styles include the Hopi white cotton manta with either blue, blue and red, or red and black borders; the woman's brown or black wool manta-dress with indigo blue diamond twill borders; the Zuni woman's manta-dress with blue embroidery; and the embroidered brown or black wool manta-dress. Dresses of this type were quite elaborate and unsurpassed in beauty. They often combined indigo blue (from the leguminous herb *Indigofera*) with red-, green-, and yellow-dyed yarns, and the embroidery combined techniques such as the historic Pueblo stitch with a variety of other stitches. The Acoma, Santa Clara, and Jemez Pueblos in New Mexico all employed embroidered designs on their clothing. Within each type of manta there are variations in style, type, and, when embroidered, decoration.

A Hopi man weaving an *atö'ö*. This type of manta or maiden's shawl was woven at various periods of time in both cotton and wool. Most were woven of cotton with a woolen border of blue; later examples featured a broad border in red. The *atö'ö* could also have blue borders or black and red borders.
Photograph by John K. Hiller.

Hopi Blue-and-Red-Bordered White Wool Manta (*atö'ö*), 1890–1920

74 x 86.5 cm

Donor: Fred Kimpton Hinchman, 535.G.833

Remarks: Also known as a "maiden's shawl," the white manta with red and blue borders undoubtedly finds its direct ancestor in the striped cotton twill-weave fabrics of the prehistoric Pueblos. The donor purchased this textile from the Fred Harvey Company at Grand Canyon, Arizona, in 1941. The original price was $15.00. This textile was purportedly a gift of a Hopi grandfather to his twelve-year-old granddaughter and was later sold to Harvey.

Analysis: This is a float, even (2/2), diagonal and diamond twill weave. It is woven of one-ply, z-spun native handspun wool for both the warp and weft. At the borders one-ply, z-spun native handspun churro wool, dyed with indigo, and three-ply, s-spun (sxs) raveled worsted wool, dyed with cochineal(?), are incorporated into the fabric.

Hopi Blue-and-Red-Bordered White Cotton Manta (*atö'ö*), 1890–1910

98 x 114 cm

Donor: Fred Kimpton Hinchman; 535.G.703

Remarks: Also known as a "maiden shawl," a manta of this type was usually made for a granddaughter by her grandfather. The donor purchased this textile from Riley Quoyavema (Sunrise), a Hopi man from the village of Mishongnovi, in 1937.

Analysis: This is a float, uneven, and diamond twill weave. The white body and red bands are 1/3 uneven twill, and the blue band is diamond twill. The warp and a portion of the weft are woven of one-ply, z-spun native handspun cotton. The diamond twill indigo blue borders are woven of one-ply, z-spun native handspun wool, and the red (dye unknown) band is woven of three-ply, s-spun, Z-twist machine-spun wool.

All mantas could be worn as shoulder blankets or wraparound dresses. Kent (1983, 55) notes that the only exception may have been the Zuni dress, which may have served only as a dress. Most of these styles were worn by women, with the garment wrapped around the body, pulled under one arm, and fastened over the opposite shoulder. This blanket-dress was held in place at the waist by a warp-faced belt or sash. It could also be worn as a shoulder blanket and, as such, served as clothing for both sexes.

In addition to the manta, rectangular fabrics were woven for waist-to-knee-length dance kilts, white or indigo blue–dyed cotton breechcloths, and shirts made of a single length of fabric folded over the shoulders with a neck opening that was cut away and self-hemmed. Those with sleeves were similarly made, but with the addition of the sleeve, which was nothing more than a small rectangular piece of fabric, folded and sewn on at the shoulder. Like the mantas, they were decorated by dyeing, embroidery, and, in a few cases, painting. Several styles of men's shoulder blankets, shaped liked mantas, were woven as gifts and presented to boys and men in rite-of-passage ceremonies. These can be identified by the natural black or brown and white wools in various combinations of float weaves, mainly in even twills.

Longer-than-wide, weft-faced woolen blankets were also manufactured. Spanish-influenced, these styles were usually patterned in banded or zoned layouts of simple or compound stripes separated by white or light tan alternating bands. Around the eighteenth century the most popular pattern was one known as the "Moki" style. Such blankets were often tightly woven from finely spun native handspun yarns or raveled fibers. The design of horizontally positioned, alternating narrow indigo blue and natural brown or black stripes is sometimes separated by similarly narrow or wide zones of white. Early examples often incorporated a type of "ticking" design along the linear edges of the white bands.

By the end of the nineteenth century extensive European contact, the tourist trade, and a wage economy led to a decline in the manufacture of Pueblo textiles. Weavers sought work outside the villages, which took them away from family and clan obligations and their looms. Pueblo weavers using traditional upright looms continue today in some manner in the Hopi villages but are rare in the New Mexico Pueblos. Those who do create woven fabrics continue to derive their inspiration from their cultural roots. Many pursue the art as an individual effort, and their work is always grounded in native thought, belief, and expression.

Santa Clara Embroidered Black Wool Manta-Dress, 1920–36

109 x 62.5 cm

Donor: Fred Kimpton Hinchman; 535.G.699

Remarks: The textile was probably woven by the Hopi and embroidered at Santa Clara Pueblo. The donor claims he saw it worn in Santa Clara, New Mexico, c. 1934–35. Upon returning to the Southwest in 1936, he saw it in a shop in Santa Fe, New Mexico, and purchased it. The embroidered band of this textile appears in a study published by H. P. Mera, Pueblo Embroidery *(1943, pl. XXIV). He noted: "Following what was obviously the golden age of embroidery design on the woolen* manta, *a rapid decline set in, beginning about 1880, until in a few years, the art itself became virtually extinct. . . . [This example] follows most closely the ideals of the old classic style, including a division into 3 zones."*

Analysis: This is a float, even (2/2) diagonal and diamond twill weave. It has a diagonal twill body with diamond twill borders. It was woven of one-ply, z-spun native handspun wool. The embroidery is of four-ply, z-spun, S-twist machine-spun, woolen yarn and two-ply, s-spun, Z-twist native handspun wool. Indigo dye is used in the diamond twill body of the manta, and the brown is a natural wool color. The embroidery yarns are aniline-dyed, and the two-ply green color has faded.

Common Threads

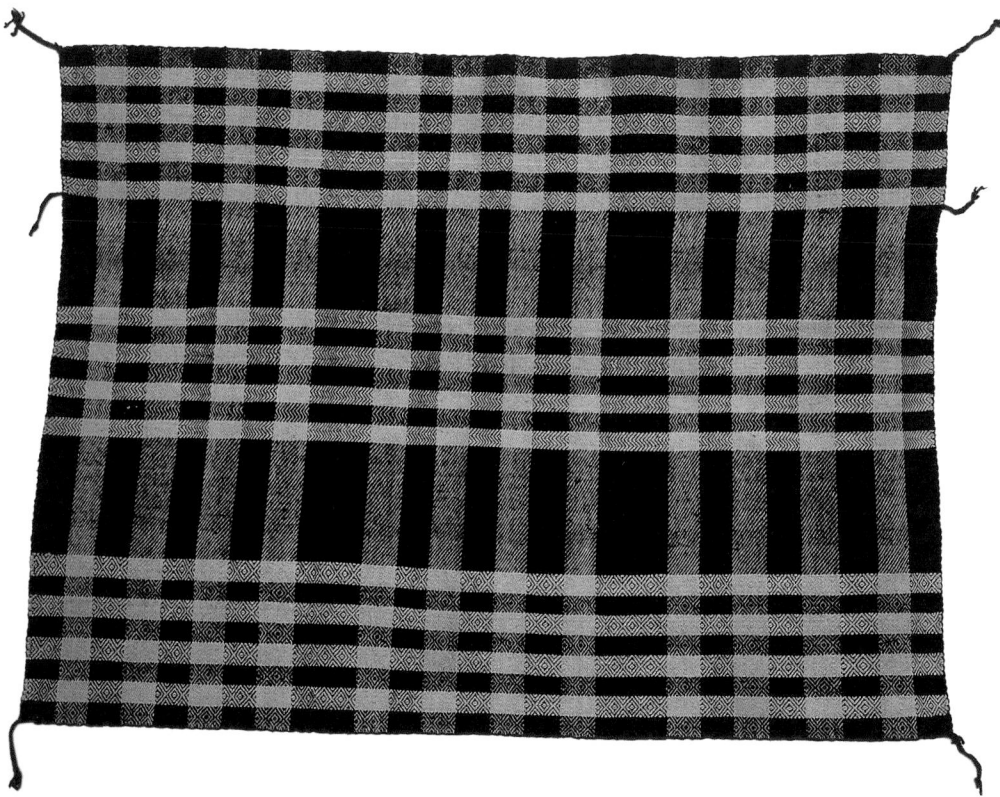

Hopi baby wrapped in a *pösalhoya*, or plaid "bachelor's blanket." This blanket was probably woven and given to the child by its father or grandfather, which is the Hopi custom. Most blankets of this type are given to a young male child during his first years of life. *Photograph by George Wharton James, Oraibi, 1902.*

Hopi Plaid Shoulder Blanket (*pösalhoya*), 1930–31

118.5 x 156 cm

Weaver: Sack-hong-va of Bakabi village

Donor: Fred Kimpton Hinchman; 535.G.552

Remarks: The donor purchased this textile at the 1931 Museum of Northern Arizona Hopi Show. The only shoulder blanket to survive in its traditional form is the plaid blanket of the Hopis. Woven of black and white or brown and white wool, a few are still made for infants and small boys. Textiles of this type are also known as "bachelor's" blankets.

Analysis: This is a float, even 2/2 (diagonal), and diamond twill (four-harness) weave. It is woven of one-ply, z-spun native handspun white and black wool. The black may have a native overdye to enhance the natural color of the wool.

Opposite, top:

Hopi Embroidered White Cotton Manta (*tu'i hi*), 1890–1910

118 x 65 cm

Donor: unknown; 1.Q.1

Remarks: This textile continues to hold the corn pollen with which it was blessed while being worn; the garment is not, however, considered sacred. It was probably woven and embroidered in one of the Hopi villages. The design of interlocking triangles worked in negative patterning has its origins in the prehistoric Pueblo period. The realistic butterfly, or poli, motifs symbolize "renewal" and fertility.

Analysis: This is a plain, balanced weave with "short rows." Both the warp and weft in this textile are one-ply, native handspun cotton. The embroidery stitches and pom-poms are of four-ply, z-spun, S-twist machine-spun woolen yarn. The embroidery technique is the Pueblo stitch. The dyes in the machine-spun yarns are all aniline, and some have faded or shifted in color.

Opposite, bottom:

Hopi Embroidered White Cotton Manta (*tu'i hi*), 1920–40

112 x 144 cm

Donor: The Wells Fargo History Museum; 91.19.29

Remarks: This manta reflects a more contemporary period in the manufacture of such woven garments. The embroidery motifs include a goat, a Shriners emblem, eagle, bee, and flowers. This textile continues to hold the corn pollen with which it was blessed while being worn; the garment is not, however, considered sacred.

Analysis: This is a plain, balanced weave with "short rows." Both the warp and weft are one-ply, z-spun native handspun cotton. The embroidery stitches and pom-poms are of four-ply, z-spun, S-twist machine-spun worsted and woolen yarns. The embroidery techniques include the Pueblo, satin, and whip stitches. The dyes in the machine-spun yarns are aniline, and some have faded and shifted in color.

Jemez Man's Shirt, 1920–30

Body: 58.5 x 54 cm; sleeves: 47 x 34.5 cm

Donor: General Charles McCormack Reeve Fund; 491.G.2404

Remarks: This shirt was purchased from Ina Sizer Cassidy, wife of artist Gerald Cassidy.

Analysis: This is a plain, weft-faced tapestry weave. It is woven of four-ply, z-spun, S-twist machine-spun cotton twine. The embroidery is of four-ply, z-spun, S-twist machine-spun woolen yarn. The red and black dyes are aniline. The pom-poms on the sleeve are made of four-ply, z-spun, S-twist machine-spun aniline-dyed yarns.

Hopi Man's Shirt, 1870–1900

135.5 x 56 cm

Donor: Fred Kimpton Hinchman; 535.G.832

Remarks: This shirt was purchased by the donor from the Fred Harvey Company and was collected for Herman Schweitzer by Pedro Muniz in 1906. The original Harvey tag remains intact on the shirt and carries the number H11028.

Analysis: This is a float, uneven diagonal twill weave. The neck opening is cut and hemmed. It is woven of one-ply, z-spun native handspun wool and two-ply, z-spun (sxs) raveled wool from cloth. Indigo-dyed yarns and yarns from the natural black color of the wool are used. The crimson red raveled material is cochineal-dyed.

Hopi Man's Shirt, 1920–25

Body: 59.6 x 52.8 cm; sleeves: 48.2 x 18.7 cm

Donor: Laura Adams Armer; 927.G.4

Remarks: This shirt was collected in the Hopi village of Oraibi, Arizona, c. 1920–25, by Juan Lorenzo Hubbell. He gave it to the donor in 1925.

Analysis: This is a plain, balanced, and brocade weave. The warp is four-ply, z-spun, S-twist machine-spun cotton twine. The weft is one-ply, z-spun native handspun wool. The brocade weave includes four-ply, z-spun, S-twist machine-spun woolen yarns in green, red, and black. The dyes are aniline.

Rio Grande Pueblo Embroidered White Cotton Kilt, 1960-70

100.5 x 64 cm

Donor: General Charles McCormack Reeve; 491.P.4118

Remarks: This garment appears to have been woven on a treadle loom. Kate Peck Kent (1983b, 23) writes, "Women in several New Mexico pueblos have begun to weave . . . on treadle looms. One weaver uses a treadle loom to produce a white cotton open-weave fabric specifically designed for embroidery." We believe that this may be one of those examples. The name Felicita Montoya is printed by hand in ink on the back of one corner of the kilt. This is probably the person who embroidered it.

Analysis: The plain, balanced weave uses the same four-ply, z-spun, S-twist machine-spun natural white cotton for warp and weft. The embroidery yarns are all aniline dyed, four-ply, z-spun, S-twist machine-spun wool yarns.

Pueblo (probably Rio Grande) Embroidered Sampler, 1934

103.5 x 35.5 cm

Donor: Fred Kimpton Hinchman; 535.G.697

Remarks: Purchased by the donor from the Maizell(?) Trading Post in Albuquerque, New Mexico, in 1936. This sampler illustrates many of the embroidery designs incorporated into Pueblo white cotton mantas and kilts and bears the initials ANM and the year 1934. Hinchman collected several of these samplers. During the 1930s Maisel was charged by the Federal Trade Commission with misleading advertising of "Indian" silver jewelry made in a mechanized shop. He did, however, employ Indians to operate his machinery. Thus, while the designs in this sampler are accurate and the Pueblo stitch technique is used, we remain uncertain about the origins of its maker.

Analysis: The embroidery is done on commercial (sack?) cloth, with four-ply, z-spun, S-twist machine-spun woolen yarn. All the dyes are aniline.

SOUTHWEST MUSEUM

Zuni Moki Style Blanket (*Bi:sale'*), 1870–80

183.5 x 112.5 cm

Donor: Fred Kimpton Hinchman; 535.G.486

Remarks: This banded-style textile was purchased from J. F. Snively, an art dealer from Pasadena, California, in 1930. It was originally identified by Hinchman as being Pueblo-made.

Analysis: This is a plain, weft-faced weave with warp lay-ins but no lazy lines. The natural white wool warp is one-ply, z-spun native handspun churro wool. The weft yarns are all one-ply, z-spun native handspun merino wools. The brown wool has possibly been overdyed, the white wool is natural, and indigo has been used to produce the blue color.

Zuni (or Navajo?) Second-Phase Chief-Style Blanket (*Bi:sale'* [Z] or *beeldléí* [N]), 1868–75

116.8 x 159.3 cm

Donor: Fred Kimpton Hinchman; 535.G.764

Remarks: We have classified this as Zuni but acknowledge that it could also be Navajo. It may be a product of intermarriage. The small size, the unevenly woven surface, the knotted corners, and the unusually formed side selvages, and an overall "feel" of a Pueblo orientation influenced our reasoning. It does, however, have embellished tassels on the corners, which is generally a Navajo trait.

Analysis: This textile is very interesting. It is a plain, weft-faced tapestry weave with warp lay-ins. The warps are one-ply, z-spun native handspun brown and white wool. The lazy lines are very unusual, resembling a wedge weave in structure, and many are considerably curved in shape. It is unevenly woven. There are seven different types of red fibers in this textile, with fourteen variations in color. The fibers include two-ply, z-spun raveled (sxs) worsted wool from cloth; one-ply, z-spun native handspun wool; three-ply, z-spun, S-twist machine-spun worsted yarn; three-ply, s-spun, Z-twist machine-spun worsted wool; four-ply, z-spun, S-twist machine-spun wool; and two-ply, z-spun, S-twist native handspun wool; six-ply, s-spun (sxs) raveled worsted wool from cloth; two-ply, z-spun, Z-twist machine-spun worsted wool; and one-ply, z-spun raveled wool from cloth. Aniline dyes, indigo, cochineal(?), and yarns spun from the natural colors of the wool define the design.

Zuni Banded Blanket (*Bi:sale'*), 1875–85

178 x 125 cm

Donor: Fred Kimpton Hinchman; 535.G.517

Remarks: Originally identified as Pueblo, this textile was purchased by the donor from an unidentified man who walked into the museum one day.

Analysis: This is a loosely woven, plain, weft-faced weave with lazy lines. The three edge warps are doubled with brown and white one-ply, z-spun native handspun merino wool. It is woven of one-ply, z-spun native handspun merino wool. Aniline- and indigo-dyed yarns and yarns spun from the natural colors of the wool define the pattern.

Wiki, a Hopi antelope priest from the village of Walpi, wearing a Hopi woven *pösaala*, c. 1890–98.
Photograph by George Wharton James.

A Brief History of Navajo Textiles

Navajo textiles are the product of individual effort and a tradition of autonomous, eclectic innovation that stresses the act of creating. Since the seventeenth century Navajo weavers have been balancing the aesthetic and the spiritual with practicality and economic reality. This is primarily because the Navajo were warriors, hunters, and part-time farmers, living in loosely organized, family-centered groups. They were autonomous bands of people whose culture was built largely on implicit behavior rather than explicit rules. There is no typical Navajo individual, and there are no special social or political classes or groups. Navajo weavers, unlike their Pueblo counterparts, responded to their craft with variety, visual flamboyance, and experimentation with dyes, fibers, and new technologies. As a result, Navajo woven fabrics incorporated ideas that extended across cultural lines, while still reflecting the weaver's own traditions.

While the Navajo were probably not weaving much in the early part of the seventeenth century, the well-established Pueblo weaving industry and trade patterns allowed them to observe the economic importance of this technology. Zuni towns were positioned at the crossroads of a major trade route that ran south to southwest, northwest toward Hopi country, and north to east to the Rio Grande Valley, Pecos Pueblo, and the southern Plains.

When Spanish oppression caused the New Mexico Pueblos to quietly rebel and compartmentalize aspects of their culture, a consequence was the decline in their loom-weaving industry. By 1639 more than half of the New Mexico Pueblos had stopped producing woven goods, and this was perhaps the catalyst for the enterprising Navajo to develop their own weaving industry. In addition, the development of a Navajo weaving industry essentially relieved the Pueblo people "of the pressure to produce mantas and blankets for the Spaniards" (Kent 1983b, 12).

By 1640 most of the Navajo settlements had churro sheep (Gregg 1844, Hill 1940), making it plausible that self-directed Navajo groups in different locations acquired their weaving skills independently at different times and perhaps from different Pueblos. Seasonal intra-group gatherings as well as family

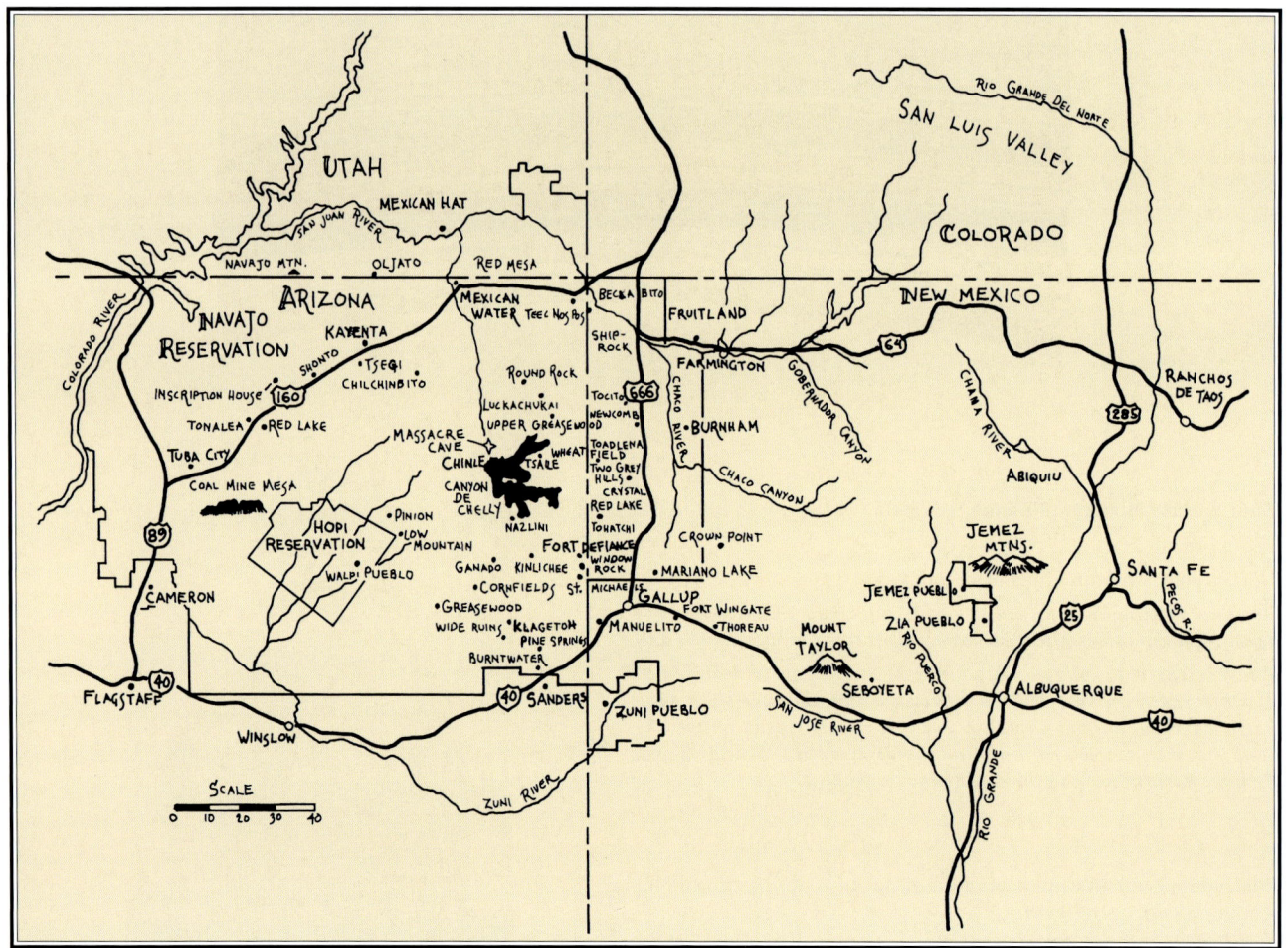

Navajo Early Classic-Style Poncho (*beeldléí* or *baghaltl'óni*), 1840–60

214.5 x 142.2 cm

Donor: Anita M. Baldwin; 630.G.65

Remarks: This is undoubtedly one of the finest Navajo textiles ever woven. The Spanish-Mexican Saltillo sarape no doubt served as a prototype for the size and length of this fabric. The design has a purely Navajo orientation.

Analysis: This is a fine, plain, weft-faced tapestry weave with lazy lines. It is woven of one-ply, z-spun native handspun churro wool and two- and three-ply, s-spun (sxs) raveled wool. The dyes are lac and indigo.

An industrious family of Navajo women demonstrating the varied processes of weaving. From left to right: a young girl spinning her cleaned and prepared wool on a spindle whorl, a woman weaving a rug on an upright loom, a very young girl carding wool, and, at the far right, a woman weaving a belt on a backstrap loom.
Photograph by George Wharton James, 1902.

Navajo Early Classic Style Blanket-Sarape (*beeldléí*), 1840–60
184.2 x 132.1 cm
Donor: Charles Fletcher Lummis; 457.G.5A
Remarks: Josiah Gregg (1844) wrote: The Navajo sarape "is of so close and dense a texture that it will frequently hold water almost equal to gum-elastic cloth. It is therefore highly prized for protection against the rains."
Analysis: This is a plain, weft-faced tapestry weave with lazy lines. It is woven of one-ply, z-spun native handspun churro wool and a two-ply, s-spun (sxs) raveled worsted wool. The dyes are indigo blue and cochineal. The white is churro wool with no dye.

exchanges may have provided the impetus for the sharing and promotion of these learned skills. Through trade of their own woven fabrics, the Navajo expanded their economic and social alliances, and an increased exchange of goods and slaves contributed to the internal consolidation of the tribe. In addition, the struggle for economic stability reinforced other Navajo values, such as personal productivity and industriousness. These are observed in social and kinship networks, particularly between family groups.

Spanish documents indicate that by 1706 the Navajo were weaving commercially and trading their textiles to the Pueblos, Utes, Comanches, Plains Indians to the north, and to the Spanish. A Spanish official reported, "They make their own cloths of wool and cotton, sowing the latter and obtaining the former from the flocks which they raise" (Hackett 1937, 3:382).

Much of our knowledge of early Navajo woven styles comes from the discovery of some of the only known examples of c. 1750–1804 garments in a shallow rock shelter, known as Massacre Cave, in northeastern Arizona. Modeled after Pueblo prototypes, these textiles included two examples of women's one- and two-piece dresses, or *biils*, as the Navajo call them, and evidence of a third. A large fragment of a blanket,

Navajo Two-Piece Woman's Dress (*biil*), 1885–1900

127 x 87 cm (both panels)

Donor: Mabel I. Aiken; 643.G.20 A, B

Remarks: Collected by Augustus and Clementine Langerberger. Navajo women wove and wore this style of garment from at least c. 1750 through 1868. After this period, following their release from the internment camp at Bosque Redondo (Fort Sumner), they began adapting a more Americanized style of clothing. This design is related to the Navajo "wedding basket" pattern. Finger-weaving is believed to have been the first technique used by the Navajo, and it seems a natural transition that designs from baskets would be transferred to loom products. As such, these original layouts and designs are considered among the oldest patterns developed by the Navajo. Juan Lorenzo Hubbell at Ganado Trading Post had weavers revive this style, c. 1885–1900. His 1902 catalogue notes: "Genuine old Bayeta [raveled wool from cloth] native wool squaw dresses, fine compact weave, elaborate patterns and very rare." The obviously incorrect assessment of the fibers in these garments as "Bayeta native wool" was no doubt a commercial tactic to make these newly woven dresses seem old to the buyer.

Analysis: These panels are plain, weft-faced tapestry weaves with lazy lines. They are woven of one-ply, z-spun native handspun wool and two-ply, s-spun raveled (sxs) wool from cloth. Aniline-red-dyed yarn and yarns spun from the natural colors of the wool define the pattern.

Navajo Woman's Manta (*beeldléí* or *biil*), 1870–85

104 x 139 cm

Donor: Mary D. Greble; 5.G.194

Remarks: This textile has four different varieties of fibers and fifteen different colors in its fabric and design. The pattern can be classified as an "eyedazzler"—unusual in the manta style.

Analysis: This is a plain, weft-faced tapestry weave with lazy lines. It has irregular warping in that sometimes two warps are wound on the frame at one time, rather than one yarn traveling back and forth over and under the frame. The warp is pink and white one-ply, z-spun native handspun wool. It is woven of one-ply, z-spun native handspun wool; four-ply, z-spun, S-twist machine-spun wool; six-ply, s-spun (sxs) raveled wool; and four-ply, s-spun (sxs) raveled American flannel wool. Aniline dyes that have shifted and faded and cochineal(?) define the pattern.

a nearly complete example in the first-phase "chief" style, and four fragmentary Spanish-style sarapes, a piece of plain-weave cloth, parts of at least two plain diagonal twill garments, and a scrap of indigo-dyed commercial cloth in plain diagonal twill were found (Wheat 1976: 421). Most were decorated with simple stripes, but a few had designs of terraced triangles and diamonds. Raveled crimson red lac-dyed and cochineal-dyed (lac and cochineal are resinous substances produced by scale insects) commercially woven cloth was among the traded material found woven into one of the fabrics. The textiles also featured finished selvage sides and ends, embellished corners, and the incorporation of "lazy lines" into the body of the fabric.

Throughout the European expansion into the Southwest, including the opening of the Santa Fe Trail in 1822, commercial trade increased, bringing with it commercial three-ply saxony wool worsted yarns, which are usually s-spun, soft, and shiny. These yarns were dyed with cochineal, vegetal materials (including indigo and madder, which produces a brown-red), and commercial dyes of the period. Other wools and Chinese silk yarns were also imported. These goods and a greater demand for commerce

Navajo Woman's Pictorial Manta (*beeldléí or biil*), 1880–1900

98 x 145 cm

Donor: R. Priscilla Beattie; 2295.G.16

Remarks: This textile was collected by the Rev. T. Cumming Beattie. Pueblo girls wore white-center mantas of this type in the late nineteenth and early twentieth centuries. They were made entirely of wool, and many of them were woven not by Pueblos, but by Navajos.

Analysis: This is a plain, weft-faced tapestry weave with lazy lines. It is woven of one-ply, z-spun native handspun merino wool. Aniline-dyed yarns and yarns spun from the natural color of the wool define the pattern.

between East and West also influenced the development of Navajo weaving. Moreover, the influx of new people and new materials into the area not only spurred innovative ideas but also promoted an increase in textile production and created a greater market for the distribution of such goods.

Early Navajo weavers continued to manufacture fabrics in the Pueblo tradition, making textiles that were wider than they were long. One such example is the brown-black-and-white-striped shoulder blanket, woven in a plain, weft-faced weave, which later evolved into the "chief" blanket. (The name has nothing to do with Navajo social structure. These blankets were so called because the style was highly prized by Plains Indian "chiefs," who acquired them for their wives and daughters [Hafen 1930; Bent 1841; Grinnell 1922, 22–28].)

The chief blanket is one of the oldest continually developed styles, and there are four identifiable phases of its development. The first phase incorporates a horizontal, zoned layout, utilizing a wide variety of alternating brown-and-white-striped grounds, with wider bands at the ends and in the center. Paired blue stripes were observed in some of the archaeological fragments of these blankets, and by 1850 the

Navajo First-Phase Chief-Style Blanket (*beeldléí* or *hanolchadi*), 1800–1850

123.1 x 208.2 cm

Donor: Fred Kimpton Hinchman; 535.G.627

Remarks: Purchased in 1933 from Mr. Braun of Los Angeles. Banded blankets of this type are rare and are documented from Southwestern archaeological sites dating to c. 1750. The pattern is believed to be one of the oldest in the Navajo design repertoire and probably predates 1750. The term hanolchadi *was recorded by Father Berard Haile (Franciscan Fathers 1910).*

Analysis: This is a plain, weft-faced tapestry weave with lazy lines. It is woven of one-ply, z-spun, native handspun churro wool. The dye is indigo blue. The brown and white yarns are spun from the natural colors of the wool.

Navajo Second-Phase Chief-Style Blanket (*beeldléí* or *hanolchadi*), 1850–65

121.9 x 172.7 cm

Donor: Anita M. Baldwin; 609.G.623

Remarks: This pattern is distinguished from the first-phase chief style by the rectangles that break up the banded layout. The oldest second-phase style is documented to c. 1851.

Analysis: This is a plain, weft-faced tapestry weave with lazy lines. It is woven of one-ply, z-spun, native handspun wool; two-ply, z-spun (sxs) raveled wool; a four-ply, z-spun (sxs) raveled wool; a three-ply, s-spun (sxs) raveled wool; and a three-ply, s-spun, Z-twist machine-spun worsted saxony wool. The warp incorporates both blue-gray and yellow three-ply, s-spun, Z-twist vegetal-dyed worsted saxony wool. Other dyes include indigo blue and cochineal. The black-brown and white are spun from the natural colors of the wool.

blue stripes were often bordered with crimson red, both from raveled cloth and from finely worsted saxony wool yarns. Shortly thereafter, small rectangles of red at the ends of the blue stripes in the blanket created a twelve-spot pattern, which came to be known as the second-phase chief style. By 1860 variants of this twelve-spot pattern began to emerge, and the motifs began to encroach on the field of alternating black and white stripes between the ends and the center panels, as if superimposed over the design plane. For fifty years Navajo weavers had incorporated terraced figures into their dresses and other weaving styles, and by 1860 a terraced diamond was placed in the center of the chief-style blanket, with quarter diamonds (right triangles) at each corner and half diamonds (isosceles triangles) within the center of the bands at each end. This style is referred to as the third phase. When the alternating brown and white stripes are overpowered by the larger diamond motifs in the design field, becoming a secondary feature of the pattern, this is referred to as the fourth phase. Variants of all these phases are observed in Navajo chief blankets after 1868.

Navajo Second-to-Third-Phase Transitional Chief-Style Blanket (*beeldléí* or *hanolchadi*), 1868–80

136 x 155 cm

Donor: Fred Kimpton Hinchman; 535.G.573

Remarks: The transitional design incorporates rectangle and triangle elements from both the second- and third-phase chief styles. The donor purchased this textile from J. F. Snively, an art dealer from Pasadena, California.

Analysis: This is a plain, weft-faced tapestry weave with lazy lines. It is woven of one-ply native handspun churro wool and three-ply, z-spun, S-twist machine-spun worsted and woolen wools. The dyes are indigo blue, and there are three colors of red. Aniline dye is evident in two of the red colors (both are faded), and cochineal(?) may have been used in a third crimson red colorant.

Ledger drawing by the southern Cheyenne artist Howling Wolf, c. 1875. Drawn during the artist's incarceration at Fort Marion, Florida, the image depicts him as a small boy with his mother. Both are dressed in their finest clothing, and Howling Wolf's mother wears a Navajo-woven third-phase chief-style blanket. *Braun Research Library, Southwest Museum;* 4100.G.23.

The continuity of this style over the decades can be traced to its importance in commerce. By 1800 these blankets had become coveted and valuable barter items. They were used to proposition for peace (NMSRC-SA: Chacon to Nava, 21 June 1800; Bancroft 1962, 268; Correll 1979, 95). They were also cited as a reason to provide the Navajo with gifts, which was the custom among the Spanish when they wanted to acquire blankets (NMSRC-SA: Salcedo to Alencaster, 23 April 1806), and used for general trade for goods, horses, and the return of slaves.

Navajo Third-Phase Chief-Style Blanket (*beeldléí* or *hanolchadi*), 1865–75
134.6 x 152.4 cm
Donor: Fred Kimpton Hinchman; 535.G.489

Remarks: This is an early third-phase style.

Analysis: This is a plain, weft-faced tapestry weave with lazy lines. It is woven of one-ply, z-spun native handspun churro wool; three-ply, z-spun, S-twist machine-spun woolen yarn; three-ply, s-spun (sxs) raveled worsted wool; and a two- and three-ply, s-spun (sxs), raveled worsted yarn. The dyes are indigo, cochineal, and a combination of indigo and rabbit brush to produce the green.

A group of Brulé women dressed in Navajo chief-style blankets and feathered headdresses at an honoring ceremony on the Brulé Sioux reservation. *Photography by J. A. Anderson, c. 1890. Courtesy of the Nebraska Historical Society.*

In addition to the chief style, the Navajo also produced a "woman's wearing blanket," which is distinguished from the chief blanket only by its slightly smaller size and narrow black and white or black and gray stripes. Here, too, the name is a misnomer derived from the assumptions of traders. There is no documentation of its exclusive use as a woman's garment (Whitaker-Bennett 1981, 68). This smaller shoulder blanket also went through a series of developmental phases similar to those undergone by the chief style. Early examples begin to appear around the 1860s.

After the two-piece *biil* replaced the earlier blue-bordered Navajo mantas, the Navajo continued to weave a similar style, which was worn as a shawl. These Pueblo-like garments had two decorated horizontally positioned panels, the most common with designs in blue on a red ground bordered in blue. The center was usually black, but occasionally one finds orange, pink, blue, or green. The designs range from terraced diamonds and triangles, zigzags, various crosses, and any combination of these, to later serrate-edged motifs of the same physical structure. Many of these shawls were made by the Navajo but sold to the Pueblos.

Navajo Chief-Style Variant Blanket (*beeldléí* or *hanolchadi*), 1885–1900

147.3 x 190.5 cm

Donor: Anita M. Baldwin; 630.G.38

Remarks: Crosses take the place of the diamonds in this third-phase variant. Crosses first began appearing in Navajo blankets c. 1862.

Analysis: This is a plain, weft-faced weave with lazy lines. It is woven of one-ply, z-spun native handspun merino wool. The dyes are aniline, with an overdye to enhance the handspun, natural black-brown wool.

Sometime between 1800 and 1830 the wider-than-long striped blankets began sharing the blanket "arena" with Navajo-made ponchos and sarapes. These sarapes, so-called because they reflect the Spanish-Mexican influence in shape and length, are weft-faced weaves woven exclusively from fine-threaded, worsted, lac- and cochineal-dyed fibers that serve as the primary ground. They are usually characterized by weblike diamond patterns, some with hollow X shapes, others with grouped zigzag lines and terraced triangles across the horizontal axis of the design plane. The red ground is often contrasted with indigo blue and native handspun white churro wool, formulating negative-positive exchanges in the overall design plane. Rare pieces incorporate muted greens and yellows in their designs. Made during the so-called Classic period (a term assigned by anthropologists), from c. 1800 to 1865, a few incorporate a tapestry slit weave structure, which allows them to be worn over the head.

The sheep that produced these garments aided the Navajos' subsistence, and the size of the herds served as an index of individual wealth. By 1840 the Navajo were also beginning to measure their wealth and status by the number of horses they acquired. That the horse had become a status symbol is evidenced by the appearance of its image not only on Navajo petroglyphs of the early 1800s but also in weaving

Navajo Third-Phase Chief-Style Woman's Wearing Blanket (*beeldléí*), 1875–85
93.3 x 134.7 cm
Donor: Fred Kimpton Hinchman; 535.G.590
Remarks: The donor purchased this textile from a Mrs. Hirshfeldt in 1932.

Analysis: This is a plain, weft-faced tapestry weave with lazy lines. It is woven of one-ply, z-spun native handspun merino wool and a four-ply, z-spun, S-twist machine-spun woolen yarn. Aniline-dyed yarns and yarns spun from the natural colors of the wool define the pattern.

designs of 1840–65. Horse songs, prayers, and origin stories began seeping into the eschatology of Navajo culture. The finely woven Classic and Late Classic small blankets woven between 1840 and 1880, equal in fineness of weave and design to their poncho and sarape counterparts, are a testament to the changes in Navajo social structure. Often referred to as "child's blankets" (another commercial misnomer in Navajo weaving terminology), blankets of this size were used as saddle covers and equestrian decoration, as doorway covers, and for a variety of other purposes.

During the period from 1860 to 1870 new yarns, dyes, cloths, and other goods being produced by American factories in the East served as catalysts for change. Design motifs and elements were undergoing subtle alterations in arrangement and position, and old patterns were reinvigorated by new color schemes. Such experiments were no doubt a response to innovations occurring throughout the Navajo weaving industry. Textile shapes were also moving from wider-than-long traditions to versions of the elongated Spanish-Mexican Saltillo sarapes and to blankets following the dimensions of standard government-issue American blankets.

Such changes were occurring, in part, because the new aniline (coal-tar derivative) dyes and additional three-ply machine-spun commercial yarns produced by American factories in Germantown, Pennsylvania, had reached the Navajo during their internment at Bosque Redondo. Between 1863 and 1878 nearly 75,000 pounds of this material were issued to the Navajo. The early colors of these yarns were very dull yellows, green-browns, reds, orange-reds, blues, and sometimes lavender-purples. In the

Navajo Chief-Style Variant Woman's Wearing Blanket (*beeldléí*), 1875–85

132 x 178 cm

Donor: Carter H. Harrison; 1520.G.6

Remarks: This blanket is in the style of a chief variant with elements of crosses and serrated diamonds that appear superimposed over a design field made up of narrow alternating black and white stripes. The term woman's wearing blanket *is no doubt of commercial origin and has acceptance in the general nomenclature of Navajo weaving. It is, however, misleading. Such blankets had a multiplicity of uses. They were distinguished from the "chief" blankets by the narrow stripes in the design field and their generally smaller size.*

Analysis: This is a plain, weft-faced tapestry weave with lazy lines. It is woven of four-ply, z-spun, S-twist machine-spun woolen yarn. The warp is four-ply, z-spun, S-twist machine-spun woolen yarn. The dyes are aniline.

early 1870s the three-ply material began to be replaced by four-ply worsted and woolen yarns produced throughout the East. Although textiles woven exclusively with machine-spun yarns are referred to as "Germantowns," the characterization is inaccurate since many factories other than those at Germantown were producing commercial yarns. By 1865 American commercial manufacturers also began producing an orange-red, aniline-dyed flannel cloth. The use of this material is often seen in Late Classic and Transitional Navajo blankets.

Additional anomalies are observed in the so-called slave blankets. From 1540 on, Navajo women and children were abducted by Spanish and Mexican soldiers on punitive expeditions into their country and taken into their households as "slaves." Those captives who continued to weave ultimately produced fabrics displaying traits of a Hispanic aesthetic and, in some cases, a modified treadle-loom warping technique, which they applied to their own upright looms. In such cases, in addition to the traditional method of using a one-ply, Z-spun warp, with a two- or three-cord selvage of various plied yarns, some "slave blankets" incorporate a two-ply warping system of Z-spun, S-twist yarns. This technique is observed in many of the textiles believed to have been created by slaves.

By 1880 innovations in Navajo weaving had increased at a rapid pace. Wedge-weave and two-faced blankets, twilled and tufted saddle blankets, and fabrics with detailed pictorials appeared with increasing frequency. American flags, trains, chickens, cows, horses, and figures of people were among the many creations. Moreover, "eyedazzler" tapestries, the product of the garish-colored three- and

Navajo Moki-Style Blanket (*beeldléí* or *nakhai bich'ídei*), 1865–75

162.5 x 116.8 cm

Donor: Charles Fletcher Lummis; 457.G.10

Remarks: The diamond motifs in this design are influenced by the Spanish-Mexican Saltillo sarape.

Analysis: This is a plain, weft-faced tapestry weave. It is woven of one-ply, z-spun native handspun churro and merino wools and one-ply, z-spun raveled worsted wool. The dyes are indigo blue and cochineal(?), and the white is both churro (warp) and merino (weft) with no dye.

Navajo Moki-Style Blanket (*beeldléí* or *nakhai bich'idei*), 1870–80

186.1 x 137.1 cm

Donor: Fred Kimpton Hinchman; 535.G.581

Remarks: The donor purchased this textile from Miss G. G. Wotkyns in 1932. According to Wotkyns, it had been brought to California fifty years earlier by a Mrs. Jewett.

Analysis: This textile is a plain, weft-faced weave with lazy lines. It is woven of one-ply, z-spun native handspun Merino wool. The dyes are indigo and aniline. The handspun natural brown-black wool may have an overdye to enhance the color.

four-ply machine-spun yarns, were quite popular from c. 1875 to 1910. Most of them had commercial cotton twine warps.

By the turn of the century, elements from Navajo religion also began appearing in textiles. Perhaps the most ubiquitous design element is a motif that resembles a backward swastika. In Navajo culture the symbol comes from sand paintings and mythology and is referred to as "whirling logs." In the Navajo language it is called "that which revolves" (*tsil no oli*) and is the fundamental basis upon which the Night Way and Feather Chant sand paintings are laid out. It designates direction and motion. Sand-painting tapestries and Yei and Yeibichai tapestries all developed from this tradition as well.

As European-style clothing increasingly replaced native woven garments, Navajo loom-woven products began changing primarily from blankets to rugs to accommodate a new market in the East. Beginning in the 1870s reservation traders such as Juan Lorenzo Hubbell, best known for his trading post at Ganado, Arizona, and his Revival-style "blanket-rugs"; C. N. Cotton, a onetime partner of Hubbell's who later moved to Gallup, New Mexico; H. B. Noel of Teec Nos Pos; and J. B. Moore of Crystal, New Mexico, were among the many entrepreneurs who opened large trading companies and introduced new ideas to Navajo weavers. Regional rug styles such as Two Gray Hills, Chinle, Teec Nos Pos, Wide Ruins, Tuba City–area storm patterns, Klagetoh, and Pine Springs, as well as a much later style that came to be known as Burnt Water, all resulted from the influences of Indian traders.

Today Navajo weaving arts are a continuing manifestation of the people and their very eclectic, autonomous lifestyle. The pace of change in the outside world has accelerated since the Victorian age, and new communication technologies have brought the world closer. These changes have had monumental effects on the lifestyle of the Navajo weaver. Young progres-

Navajo Moki-Style Blanket (*beeldléí* or *nakhai bich'idei*), 1885–1900

193.6 x 138.4 cm

Donor: Mrs. Teresa C. Fulford; 1842.G.28

Remarks: This blanket is identical in design to another example in the museum's collection (288.L.1). Another one of this design recently sold at a May 1998 auction at Sotheby's in New York. This one was originally purchased by Frank E. Curtis in c. 1900 from Lorenzo Hubbell at Hubbell's Trading Post, Ganado, Arizona.

Analysis: The textile is a plain, weft-faced tapestry weave with lazy lines. It is woven of four-ply, z-spun, S-twist machine-spun woolen yarn. The warp is four-ply, s-spun, S-twist machine-spun woolen yarn. All the dyes are aniline.

Navajo Moki-Style Blanket (*beeldléí* or *nakhai bich'ídei*), 1875–85

200 x 138.5 cm

Donor: Riley Quoyavema (Sunrise); 288.L.1

Remarks: This Moki is identical in design to another blanket in the museum's collection (1842.G.28). This one was donated to the museum in 1942 by Riley Quoyavema (Sunrise), a Hopi man from the village of Mishongnovi. This pattern is thought to have been originated by a weaver either employed by, or living near, the Hubbell Trading Post at the turn of the century. Although the pattern has not been traced to existing paintings in Hubbell's "rug study," it is believed that blankets with this design were regularly sold to tourists.

Analysis: This is a plain, weft-faced weave with lazy lines. It is woven of a one-ply, z-spun native handspun merino wool; a two- and three-ply, z-spun (sxs) raveled wool; a three-ply s-spun (sxs) raveled worsted wool; and a four-ply, z-spun, S-twist machine-spun woolen yarn. The dyes are aniline, indigo, and cochineal(?).

sivists seem to thrive on the changes, while older traditionalists are somewhat resistant to them. The civil rights movement, including the American Indian Movement; the social and political efforts of the Native American Rights Fund; and new federal laws such as the 1990 Indian Arts and Crafts Act and the 1991 Native American Graves Protection and Repatriation Act have reinforced renewed pride in Native American ethnic heritage and identity. Tourism and commerce on the reservation, changes in the family structure and in gender roles, and new job opportunities have also contributed to transformations in the traditional way of life and to new trends in weaving (Hedlund 1992).

The Navajo weaving industry might be characterized today as many flourishing enterprises, with the Navajo weaver and her family as business owners. Weavers draw on their own ideas and experiences. They take the best of what they want and reject what they don't want in terms of ideas and materials. But beyond simple innovation and adaptation of borrowed ideas, which are reshaped into a purely Navajo product, today's weavers, like their ancestors, are resourceful and independent. While it is true that they respond to the marketplace, they never forget the cultural roots from which their art has grown. In the virtuoso textiles they weave, they continually honor that which has gone before, while still reflecting their own experiences and hopes. Modern connoisseurs have also taken a new approach to collecting. Unlike their predecessors, they recognize the creator as well as the creation.

Navajo Moki-Style Blanket (*beeldléí* or *nakhai bich'ídei*), 1875–85

174 x 119 cm

Donor: Fred Kimpton Hinchman; 535.G.642

Remarks: This textile was purchased by the donor in 1934 from Mr. Miller, who owned a shop on Wilshire Boulevard in Los Angeles.

Analysis: This is a plain, weft-faced tapestry weave with lazy lines. It is woven of one-ply, z-spun native handspun merino wool. The dyes are indigo and aniline.

Navajo Late Classic-Style Small Blanket (*beeldléí*), 1868–78

127 x 84 cm

Donor: Carter H. Harrison; 1520.G.11

Analysis: This is a plain, weft-faced tapestry weave with lazy lines. It is woven of one-ply, z-spun, native handspun wool; three-ply, z-spun, S-twist machine-spun woolen yarn; and one-, two-, and three-ply z-spun (sxs) raveled worsted wools. The dyes are three shades of indigo blue (light to dark); cochineal(?); and aniline green, salmon, and red-orange. The white and gray have no dye.

Navajo Late Classic-Style Small Blanket
(*beeldléí*), 1868–80

123.8 x 98.7 cm

Donor: Fred Kimpton Hinchman; 535.G.572

Remarks: Originally identified by Hinchman as a double saddle blanket. In 1927 Amsden wrote in the SWM archival records: "This is the best evidence for the Army Uniform theory I've ever seen yet," alluding to the fact that some of the raveled wools appeared to be from army uniforms.

Analysis: This is a plain, weft-faced tapestry weave. It is woven of one-ply, z-spun native handspun merino wool and two- and three-ply, z-spun (sxs) raveled worsted wools. The dyes are indigo blue, cochineal(?)-dyed raveled reds; aniline-dyed raveled worsted green; aniline-dyed raveled worsted yellow-tan (shifted to orange-gold); and aniline-dyed raveled worsted blue (which has faded). The white is handspun merino wool with no dye.

Navajo Blanket (*beeldléí*), 1875–85

189.2 x 132 cm

Donor: Sylvia Rindge Adamson Neville for The Adamson Companies; 2087.G.8

Remarks: The collector was Frederick Hastings Rindge. The technology and dyes in this textile indicate that it may be a "slave" blanket. Such blankets were woven by Navajos who had been captured by Spaniards and lived in Spanish households. A "slave" blanket usually reflects the Hispanic preferences in color and warping techniques but is woven on an upright rather than a horizontal treadle loom.

Analysis: This is a plain, weft-faced weave with lazy lines. The wool is crimped and stiff in texture. It has a cotton warp. Each warp consists of two strands of four-ply, z-spun, S-twist machine-spun cotton, plied together S-twist. Dyes include faded aniline dyes in purple, red, pink, green, magenta, and pea green.

Navajo Wedge-Weave Blanket (*beeldléí*), 1880–90

198 x 153 cm

Donor: Fred Kimpton Hinchman; 535.G.811

Remarks: This textile was purchased by the donor from a Mr. Gray of Laguna Beach, California, in 1939.

Analysis: This weave structure is also known as "pulled warp." In the wedge-weave structures the lazy lines are used to start the "wedges." The textile is woven of one-ply, z-spun native handspun wool. Aniline-dyed yarns and yarns spun from the natural colors of the wool help define the design.

Navajo Large Eyedazzler Tapestry (*beeldléí*), 1885–1910

223.5 x 146 cm

Donor: Fred Kimpton Hinchman; 535.G.514

Analysis: This is a plain, weft-faced tapestry weave with lazy lines. The warp is three-ply, z-spun, S-twist machine-spun cotton twine. The weft is woven of four-ply, z-spun, S-twist machine-spun woolen yarn. All of the dyes are aniline.

Navajo Pictorial Tapestry (*beeldléí*), 1875–1900

236.2 x 116.8 cm

Donor: Sylvia Rindge Adamson Neville for The Adamson Companies; 2087.G.35

Remarks: This tapestry was heavily influenced by the design and layout of the Spanish-Mexican Saltillo sarape. In addition to the long length of the fabric and the central diamond motif, there are pictorial elements of bows and arrows derived from Navajo sand-painting motifs.

Analysis: This is a fine and tightly woven, plain, weft-faced tapestry weave with lazy lines. The warp is three-ply, z-spun, S-twist machine-spun cotton twine, and the weft is all four-ply, z-spun, S-twist machine-spun woolen yarns.

Navajo Eyedazzler Blanket (*beeldléí*), 1885–1900

214 x 146 cm

Donor: Fred Kimpton Hinchman; 535.G.591

Remarks: This is one of the few blankets in existence that incorporates a "Spider Woman hole." Amsden (1934, 102) quoted the Ethnologic Dictionary *(Franciscan Fathers 1910): "It is generally stated that this weave had to be occasionally resorted to avoid overdoing weaving." There is no real evidence, however, to support this theory. There have been only a handful of textiles with Spider Women holes woven in Navajo weaving history. Amsden claimed he had seen only three, including this example. The design might be characterized as an "eyedazzler," and this particular style was favored by C. N. Cotton. One of similar design and character appears in his 1896 catalogue.*

Analysis: This is a plain, weft-faced, loosely woven tapestry weave with lazy lines. A small one-inch opening created by a slit tapestry weave, called a Spider Woman hole, is located within the body of the fabric. It is woven of one-ply, z-spun native handspun merino wool. The dyes are aniline.

Navajo Pictorial Blanket (*beeldléí*), 1885–1900

187.3 x 131.4 cm

Donor: Sylvia Rindge Adamson Neville for The Adamson Companies; 2087.G.63

Remarks: Collected by Frederick Hastings Rindge. Cows (in this example, with brands) and other domesticated animals were popular themes with many Navajo weavers before 1900.

Analysis: This is a plain, weft-faced tapestry weave with lazy lines. It is woven of one-ply, z-spun native handspun wool. The unusual warp is of one ply, z-spun native handspun wool in a natural brown and two types of machine-spun cotton twine; one a three-ply, z-spun S-twist and the other, a four-ply, z-spun S-twist. Aniline-dyed yarns and yarns spun from the natural colors of the wool define the design.

Navajo Pictorial Saddle Blanket (*ak' idah' nii*), 1885–1900

62.5 x 93 cm

Donor: Joseph Keppler; 1409.G.219

Remarks: Single-style saddle blankets that are as highly decorated as this one are also referred to as Sunday saddle blankets. This one also has an "eyedazzler" pattern. By the early 1800s Navajos had begun to measure their wealth and status by the number of horses they acquired. Horse songs, prayers, and origin stories began seeping into the eschatology of Navajo culture.

Analysis: This is a plain, weft-faced tapestry weave with lazy lines. It is woven of one-ply, z-spun native handspun wool; four-ply, z-spun, S-twist machine-spun worsted and woolen yarns. The fringe was added without knots but is heavily damaged.

Navajo *Yei* Tapestry (*beeldléí*), 1925–31

171.4 x 105.4 cm

Donor: Fred Kimpton Hinchman; 535.G.533

Remarks: This "corn stalk Yei" pictorial tapestry is the Navajo version of the "tree of life." The bow-and-arrow pictorial elements are derived from Navajo sand paintings.

Analysis: This is a plain, weft-faced tapestry weave with lazy lines. It is woven of one-ply, z-spun native handspun wool. Aniline-dyed yarns and yarns spun from the natural colors of the wool define the pattern.

Navajo *Yei* Tapestry (*beeldléí*), 1930–40

214 x 123 cm

Donor: Leda R. Griswold; 1225.G.27

Remarks: This tapestry is unusual because the Yei figures run warp-wise, rather than against the warp. The feathers in the headdress are woven in a technique similar to the wedge weave.

Analysis: This is a plain, weft-face tapestry weave, without lazy lines. It is woven of one-ply, z-spun native handspun wool. Aniline-dyed yarns and yarns spun from the natural colors of the wool define the pattern. The side and end cords are braided together at the corners.

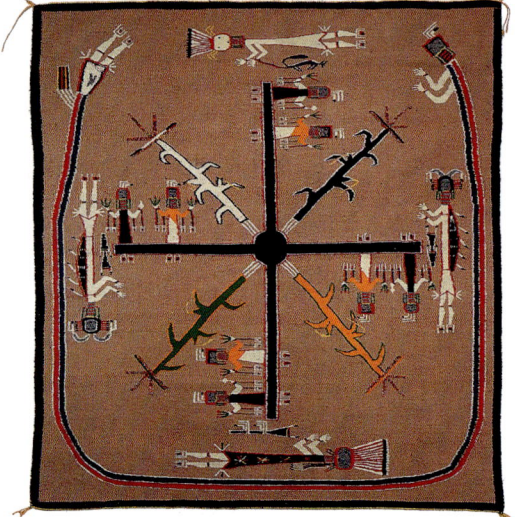

Navajo Sand-Painting Tapestry (*beeldléí* or *tsil no oli*), 1925–35

176 x 168 cm

Donor: Fred Kimpton Hinchman; 535.G.598

Remarks: The Navajo refer to this pattern as tsil no oli, *or that which revolves. The primary motif in the pattern designates direction. The design is from their Night Way Chant. This tapestry is illustrated in Amsden's* Navajo Weaving: Its Technic and History *(1934, pl. 54). He wrote: "Of late years, and probably under similar monetary inspiration, blankets embodying whole sand paintings have appeared on the market. . . . Like the Yei blankets, they are but an invasion of the temple by the money changers, although often possessed of both artistic and ethnologic value." When this example was woven, weavers were defying the belief that they would develop a grave illness or even blindness. In general, the Navajo believed that the sacred symbols indelibly woven into a tapestry robbed an actual sand-painting ceremony of its power and therefore its effectiveness. The Yei figures in this tapestry symbolize Navajo holy beings. The manner in which the wool is processed suggests that this textile may have been woven by a member of the Klah family.*

Analysis: This is a plain, weft-faced tapestry weave with lazy lines. It is woven of one-ply, z-spun native handspun wool. Aniline-dyed yarns and yarns spun from the natural colors of the wool define the pattern.

Navajo Early Crystal-Style Rug (*beeldléí*), 1895–1911

158 x 96.5 cm

Donor: Southwest Museum Acquisition Fund; 47.P.259

Remarks: Designs of this type were promoted by John B. Moore of the Crystal Trading Post in New Mexico. This design was featured in his 1911 catalogue (pl. XXX) as a special design and weave by "Bi-leen Al-pai-bi-zha-Ahd." It was a Moore ER 20 class and was priced from $.90 to $1.00 per square foot or $20.00 to $23.50, according to size.

Analysis: This is a plain, weft-faced tapestry weave with lazy lines. It is woven of one-ply, z-spun native handspun wool. Aniline-dyed yarns and yarns spun from the natural colors of the wool define the pattern.

Navajo Early Crystal-Style Rug (*beeldléí*), 1900–1911

196 x 132 cm

Donor: Fred Kimpton Hinchman; 535.G.771

Remarks: Purchased in 1934 by the donor from J. F. Snively, an art dealer from Pasadena, California. The design was promoted by J. B. Moore of the Crystal Trading Post in New Mexico. It was originally omitted from Moore's 1911 catalogue but has been identified as plate XVII, which was designed by Hasteen Yazzie be Eh-son. The rug features very stylized "Spider Woman" crosses.

Analysis: This rug is a loosely woven, plain, weft-faced tapestry weave, with lazy lines. It is woven of one-ply, z-spun native handspun wool. Aniline-dyed yarns and yarns spun from the natural colors of the wool define the pattern.

Navajo Pictorial Rug (*beeldléí*), 1900–1920

269.2 x 137.1 cm

Donor: General Charles McCormack Reeve Fund; 491.P.3457

Remarks: This pictorial depicts cattle with brands, a dog with a collar (which Bill Malone of Hubbell's Trading Post notes is a sure sign of non-Indian affiliation), pigs, chickens, a mountain lion (puma), a school house with two schoolchildren, white men with hats, white women, and various numbers (one of which may indicate the date 1902). The textile incorporates the name Charles (Chas.) Ashcroft of Fruitland, New Mexico. This may be a specialty order rug. It was purchased by the museum from John Clay in 1959.

Analysis: This is a plain, weft-faced weave with lazy lines. It is woven of one-ply, z-spun native handspun wool. The dyes are aniline and vegetal (and portions appear to have been hand-painted in brown dye?). Much of the tan-gray-brown ground is blended and carded wool with no dye.

Navajo Transitional Blanket-Rug (*beeldléí*), 1885–1902

207 x 162.5 cm

Donor: George Wharton James; 421.G.1501

Remarks: James (1914, 137, fig. 197) noted: "This was taken up from the floor of my living-room, where it has been in constant daily use for between seventeen and eighteen years. In color it is as rich and striking as the day I purchased it on the Little Colorado River, some fifty miles or so from the Santa Fe Railway at Canyon Diablo." This is classified in today's terminology as an "eyedazzler." James referred to it as an "outline" blanket.

Analysis: This is a plain, weft-faced tapestry weave with lazy lines. It is woven of one-ply, z-spun native handspun wool. The dyes are aniline.

In Search of a Weaving Aesthetic

The Impact of Cultural Interaction on Pueblo and Navajo Textiles

One can be unabashedly in love with Navajo and Pueblo textiles without knowing anything about the people who wove them. On the surface their beauty is dramatic, but closer examination reveals the strength, the individual character, and the culture of their makers. Yet, among early nineteenth- and twentieth-century preservationists who adopted the cause of "saving" American Indian heritage, the notion that it might be valuable to learn more about the people who produced these artifacts was absurd. These collectors preferred the world of native art to that of native people. As a result, our knowledge of early Navajo and Pueblo textiles is limited. What knowledge we have is attributed to those who found it easier to see these objects outside the context of their culture. As a result, we continue to search for the common threads that stimulated Navajo and Pueblo weaving, seeking to discover what motivated these people, through difficult times, to create the virtuoso tapestries that now reside in public and private collections throughout the world.

Historical Background

The nineteenth century was witness to tremendous social, economic, and political transformations, not just for indigenous Southwesterners, but for all Native Americans and for people all over the world. It was a time of growth and change. In the early 1800s the American republic was young and poor, and its future was uncertain. The Pueblo and Navajo were supporting themselves through hunting and gathering, horticulture, or both. European immigrants were flooding into the new land, seeking their own livelihood in whatever way they could. Wars were fought; territories were ceded. By the close of the nineteenth century the United States had grown rich and powerful, extending its borders across the North American continent. American expansionism, coupled with warfare and disease, had decimated the Indian populations, and the government was determined to "civilize" the tribes that survived.

It was these early Euro-American intruders—beginning with sixteenth-century Spanish garrisons, followed by American military men, missionaries, painters, adventurers, and traders—who provided the first accounts of Indian lifestyles and art. Foreigners who had contact with the native inhabitants of the region acquired Navajo and Pueblo textiles for a variety of reasons, ranging from idle curiosity to more aggressive motives.

For many, these objects were "souvenirs" of exotic encounters. The letters and diaries of these individuals offer the first hints, at least in written form, of a native art tradition and aesthetic. While the accuracy of what has been written is sometimes at variance with established facts, a secondary, and probably unintended, value is that they unwittingly tell of a non-native aesthetic as well, giving us a sense of why people outside the Navajo and Pueblo communities were drawn to collect their weaving art.

Plains and Plateau Indian people, for instance, coveted the tightly woven fabrics for comfort and warmth, as replacements for their own dwindling buffalo robes, and as status symbols. Many of the c. 1820–50 Euro-American observers told of the classical beauty and fineness of weave exhibited by Navajo textiles. They referred to the unique cultural character of Pueblo-manufactured tapestries. Some journalists identified patterns, while others vividly described the colors of the textiles. These accounts tell us as much about the attitudes and ideas of the writers as they do about the native aesthetic they were attempting to describe. Intertwined with these accounts were suggestions of the rapid changes taking place in the Arizona and New Mexico territories after the American occupation in 1848.

American military action and the expanding territorial quest of American settlers in the Southwest unfortunately began to have devastating effects on the Navajo and Pueblo. As rapid as the movement of Euro-Americans into Indian territory was the response of the American military to the Indians' efforts to protect their land. Soon the Navajo and some of their neighbors lost free access not only to their land but to the animals that provided their livelihood as well. Beginning in 1862, more than eight thousand Navajo were rounded up, their flocks of sheep were slaughtered, their agricultural fields were destroyed, and they were made to walk several hundred miles to the alkali-impregnated soil of *Hweeldi*, or Fort Sumner (commonly called Bosque Redondo), where they were incarcerated until 1868. Many died of dysentery; others contracted syphilis from the army garrison (Bailey 1964 and 1970, Thompson 1976, Navajo Community College 1973). "Reservations"—which were woefully impoverished land areas, offering little opportunity—were later set aside for American Indian use.

While the Pueblos were also affected by these invasive immigration patterns and military campaigns, their experiences varied from region to region and from group to group. The Hopi people in Arizona were generally left alone because of their isolation on high, uninviting mesa tops, and their seemingly uncultivable sandy soil. They posed a threat neither to those seeking land nor to the military sent to protect the immigrants. As a result, in 1882 President Chester A. Arthur officially set aside the land the Hopi had been occupying for their continued use.

As the American occupation of the Southwest began, Pueblo people in New Mexico were allowed to remain in their villages, seemingly free of the paternalistic shackles of the U.S. government because of its continuing indecision regarding what constituted an "Indian." In 1869, in *United States v. Lucero* (1 N.M. 422, 438, 442 [1869]; Cohen 1942, 2n. 2), it was decided the Pueblos could not be "Indians" because they were "honest, industrious, and law abiding citizens" and "a people living for three centuries in fenced abodes and cultivating the soil for the maintenance of themselves and families." The New Mexico territorial authorities, then only an agency of the federal government, generally accorded the Pueblo people the same status as other municipal corporations in the area. Unfortunately, the conditions under which they lived dramatically changed when New Mexico opted for statehood in 1913.

The Pueblos' status as a people was challenged, and control over their territory was relinquished to a government that had had very little contact with them and that wanted their land. The United States Federal Indian Bureau launched a campaign to malign the Pueblo by compiling reports of debauchery, continual dancing, drunkenness, and an unsavory communal life. The bureau eventually convinced the Supreme Court that the earlier argument that they were *not* "Indians" was based on erroneous reports. The New Mexico Enabling Act, followed by *United States v. Sandoval* in 1913, upheld the government's right to extend federal control, thereby depriving the Pueblos of the right to own land and of their claim to citizenship, which had originally been granted in 1869.

In essence, what was occurring was a confrontation between two diametrically opposed social and economic orders. Americans seemed to view the cohesion and harmony of the New Mexico Pueblos in decidedly negative terms: they saw these communities as static and out of touch with modern life and greatly in need of reform. The strong Pueblo belief in their own traditions led to an equally insistent rejection of many American attitudes and an attempt to remain politically and economically independent. Thus, the ability of both groups to interact successfully was hampered for many decades to come.

The Impact of American Expansionism

The loss of territory and self-determination affected all aspects of Pueblo and Navajo culture. The artistic development of each group was impacted on two levels: an ideological one and a material and economic one. The Navajo and Pueblo responses to these events led to a different outcome for each culture.

At the ideological level, the Pueblo people pretended to compromise by appearing to accept American ideas of modernization. While they adopted features that would make their lives easier, they continued to practice their indigenous religion and other customs and kept them sequestered from scrutiny. This strategy had been employed since the Spanish period. Their tenacity in maintaining this separateness left no doubt that the Pueblos' primary allegiance was to native ceremonial life and social custom.

Pueblo arts and crafts, including weaving, remained inextricably linked to this cultural system. Garments were woven to identify important members of the community; to honor individuals who were to be initiated into various hunting, war, and ceremonial societies; for communal dances; for rites of passage such as birth and marriage; and as reciprocal gifts. Moreover, garments woven exclusively for these purposes were not subject to experimentation with design or color. There were few innovations, and the changes that did occur were subtle and had no effect on the sacredness or meaning of Pueblo ritual. For example, replacement of native cotton by commercial cotton string was gradual, and commercially made fabrics eventually supplanted native woven ones.

Changes were first prompted by the *encomienda* system (under which the Spanish crown granted control of a parcel of land and its Indian inhabitants to an individual, who could exact tribute from the Indians and was in turn required to protect them and instruct them in the Christian faith), and the need for additional alterations came when these closely knit communities were confined to reservations. Cotton crops dwindled, and the weaving industry among the Rio Grande pueblos began to "starve." By the time sheep raising became a viable enterprise, many of the eastern pueblos had ceased their production of woven goods. Blanket and manta manufacture continued, however, in the Hopi villages, at Zuni, and occasionally, until the early 1800s, at Acoma, Laguna, Santa Clara, and Tesuque. Thereafter, most of the New Mexican villages requiring woven cotton garments acquired them from the Hopi in Arizona.

Through the nineteenth and into the twentieth century, the male weavers at Hopi cooperated within their highly stable and long-established social and religious orders. As a result, the designs and styles of their fabrics continued to reflect their intended cultural uses. Moreover, weavers were highly esteemed for their skills. Although a few unorthodox pieces were produced, the manufacture of Pueblo textiles generally responded to cultural needs—reflecting native thought, belief, and expression—rather than commercial ones. The aesthetic nature of these tapestries exemplifies a model of sharing and cooperation, and although they may have been created by individuals, they articulate communal sensibilities.

The disruption of their traditional way of life elicited a much different artistic response from the Navajo. Despite the tragic consequences of their internment at Bosque Redondo, their world view allowed them to be more receptive to the Americans, who valued, above all, mastery of the material realm and the earthly rewards resulting therefrom. In the Navajo world, art is a part of everyday life, and the creation of beauty represents health, harmony, and happiness. Moreover, beauty, or *hozho,* is the most desirable form of experience and a normal pattern of nature. There are guidelines for maintaining such a quality in life, but no rigid cultural dictates. Supported by the cultural sanctions of Spider Woman and motivated by their quest to beautify their world through art, the Navajo seemed better prepared to accept this new American culture and its notions of economic freedom, human rights (as opposed to obligations), and evolutionary social progress.

Furthermore, the flexibility of their culture allowed weavers the freedom to incorporate change into their art. The cultural value of a Navajo textile is the representational power it carries for the weaver; it lies in the process of its creation, not in the final product or its preservation. This philosophy allowed weavers to sell or trade their work without hesitation. Weaving was a practical necessity as well, and the primary incentive for Navajo weavers was the monetary support it offered their families. Beyond the commercial aspects, however, weaving provided a link to their heritage.

Enterprising merchants and reservation traders were creating a new consumer market in the eastern United States for the Navajo. Their weaving industry began to reflect the autonomous efforts of weavers striving to meet the demands of a commerce-driven American market. This interplay between textile production and the economic dimensions of intercultural exchange was not new for the Navajo. In the early 1700s they ventured far beyond their boundaries to trade at Indian and Spanish gatherings. So it seemed reasonable, during the early years of American occupation, to explore new markets for their art. There is no doubt that the Navajo welcomed the economic opportunities.

The Navajo continued to experiment with new resources and a new way of life. By the turn of the century weavers, responding to ideas suggested by traders, began making floor rugs, portieres (door hangings), and other functional and decorative products sought after by Americans. Weaving styles and the types of finished products reflected a willingness to adapt to the demands of modern reservation life. Thus, as one century ended and another began, the lack of freedom afforded by the Navajos' physical environment stood in contrast to their highly expressive, freely evolving art.

By contrast, the Pueblo seemed reluctant to commercialize their weaving industry, except in trade with other Pueblos and occasionally with other Indians, such as the Navajo. There were a few attempts by "maverick" weavers to create products for the American commercial market, but they met with little success. Moreover, as a rule, Pueblo individualists who ventured beyond accepted communal behavior met with severe reprimands within their villages. Yet, despite these stringent cultural norms, a reluctance to experiment with new weaving designs and colors may not have been a significant factor in the continuing development of the industry.

By 1900 most of the eastern Pueblos had greater access to imported machine-woven goods, including brightly colored shawls and blankets, and had ceased to weave. New material possessions seemed to signal a change in the economy. Textile production was reduced to an "as-needed" basis, lessening the need for weavers' skills and greatly reducing their role and status. The dwindling number of weavers mandated a collective acceptance of commercially made fabrics for daily wear and, eventually, as a substitute for handwoven garments in ceremonies and rituals. The future of the Pueblo weaving industry seemed to rest with the Hopi and, unfortunately, many of the Hopi men were no longer able to support their families through this craft alone. They, too, eventually succumbed to the need for work outside their villages.

The Role of Culture and Personal Experiences in Defining a Native Aesthetic

Throughout Pueblo history cultural experiences have helped to define individual artists' works and aesthetics. Personal as well as cultural interactions gave weavers the foundation and freedom to create. Many contemporary weavers emphasize that their art is not just superficial decoration but has meaning. As it is today, so it was in the past. Weaving was a ceremony unto itself, and there were songs, prayers, and thoughts about the history behind the piece being created. Each weaver added his or her personal power and energy to the process.

Weavers past and present have employed the same imagery and styles because they have meaning and purpose. The meaning of these tapestries can best be understood when they are viewed in relationship to the period in which they were woven. As issues of violation and intrusion became significant concerns in the lives of the Pueblo people, this was reflected in their art. Adverse events gave new direction to Pueblo weaving, but today these themes are balanced with a positive celebration of the art form. Today designs and styles are conceptualized in a different way, and they have meaning that resonates beyond the Pueblo artist's community; they have universal expression. As Hopi-Tewa artist Dan Namingha once noted, Pueblo art begins with uncertainty, which is part of the creative journey and the evolution of the art. When the meaning changes, so does the art; it is in continual evolution (1994, untitled lecture, Southwest Museum). Perhaps this is sufficient explanation for how Pueblo weaving has been passed on through the generations.

The creative process of Navajo weaving, from the weaver's perspective, is also divorced from how things are manipulated and exploited in life. Weaving combines emotional, moral, and intellectual expressions. Navajo textiles are to be respected and admired for the satisfaction and balance that are restored in the weaver's life each time she works at the loom. The process of weaving a design by manipulating the warp and weft re-creates the weaver's experiences as a Navajo and an artist. A weaver will tell you, "I think about it, then the thread forms the design as it pulls me through the loom." For the Navajo, as for the Pueblo, weaving is an art that serves to unify the individual with his or her world and experiences.

The artistic achievement represented by the blankets, rugs, and wall tapestries produced by the Navajo and Pueblo since 1900 was clearly not accomplished by slavishly producing what traders and tourists wanted, nor by conforming to the traditions of the past. Woven tapestries have retained their cultural importance because weavers reached beyond their cultural limits and created things that not only brought psychological and social satisfaction but that were also useful and that provided economic stability. Just as their ancestors did throughout the seventeenth, eighteenth, and nineteenth centuries, weavers today continue to reshape their industry.

Early Collectors of Navajo and Pueblo Textiles

In considering the flourishing creative forces of the Navajo and Pueblo cultures today, one might recall the grim view of the future of the American Indian that prevailed a century ago. It was thought that the Indian way of life would soon die out. Concerned non-Indian citizens' groups began to respond to this concern. Their efforts, however, were dedicated not to saving a people, but to preserving their unwritten history. Barely trained "ethnologists" turned to collecting the things Indians made as a means of salvaging their heritage. Few questioned the notion that the sophisticated products in their possession were made by people they had characterized as "savage."

Equally interesting is the fact that, under whatever "flag" the endeavor for cultural preservation was carried out, both the products of Indian creativity and their acquisition by non-Indians helped to formulate a model for museum ethnology in the United States. At the turn of the century, as the theme of a dying American Indian race pervaded the art and literature of the period, Anglo-American men and women were challenged by their passions and their egos not only to preserve the artifacts of Indian culture but to build monuments to their collecting tastes. For many, this challenge became a bugle call to "get the goods before they're gone." Within members of the priestly class of scholar-collectors, there often lurked a dark side, the commercial conquistador. Although trained museum professionals of the era might disagree with this view, a competitive strategy for acquiring materials was as important to building a collection as a critical, trained eye. There were many others "in the field," all vying for their share of the spoils.

Despite arguments that museums were working in the interests of science and had no commercial motives, there is little evidence of a "scientific method" at the turn of the century. Collectors gathered things that looked old, rare, or unusual, and the idea was to purchase them regardless of their provenance. Too often objects were found in "curio" shops or in granny's attic. More to the point, very little was known about the objects that were acquired. Adding to the uncertainty was the prevailing assumption that if an object was collected in, say, a Hopi village, it must have been made by the Hopi. The fallacy of that thinking has compounded the errors in museum archives for decades.

Even more interesting, however, was the Indian response to these early salvage expeditions. The "vanishing Indian" was making a thriving comeback as a purveyor of "traditional" goods—objects they were happy to manufacture for the eager collector (Fane 1991, 23). "Revivals" began to play an active role in providing collectors with objects related to the past. If an object was not available for purchase, traders and Indian entrepreneurs were willing to encourage a native artist to make a replica for the collector. For their part, the Navajo weavers were ready to oblige by creating designs that would appeal to collectors.

Tourism brought about changes not only in the

Navajo Early Classic-Style Poncho (*beeldléí* or *baghaltl'óni*), 1840–60

209.5 x 134.5 cm

Donor: Charles Fletcher Lummis; 457.G.1

Remarks: Purchased from Martin de Valle's son, c. 1890. De Valle was the governor of Acoma Pueblo and purportedly purchased this textile from a Navajo war leader thirty years before his son sold it to Lummis.

Analysis: This is a plain, weft-faced tapestry weave with lazy lines. It is woven of a one-ply, z-spun native handspun churro wool and two- and three-ply (sxs), s-spun raveled worsted wools. The dyes are indigo blue and lac. The white is churro wool with no dye. A slit tapestry weave forms the poncho opening.

competition for ethnographic objects but also in the material culture of the people producing them. The influx of vacationers to the reservation made the acquisition of textile "souvenirs" much easier. Prices were raised, although very few weavers reaped the benefits. Unfortunately, as museum ethnologists soon discovered, popular demand made it difficult to sustain any notion of a traditional craft. Fast production and cheap imitations were becoming the norm, and it was becoming hard to find quality materials with their creators.

As the competition for objects increased, a few ethnologists were determined to go beyond what they had learned from books, writings, and the objects themselves. They sought out the unknown quantities of unrecorded and often unattainable materials by locating native "informants." By establishing a close working relationship with Indian communities, these ethnologists became privileged interpreter-translators of Indian culture. But, interestingly, the information they gathered from the native people generally took a backseat to the immense personal pride they took in detailing events of their lives "in the field" and recording their purchases in Indian villages, writing reports, diaries, correspondence, and the like. These documents go far beyond simple record keeping. They invite the reader to participate in the mental and physical processes of collecting and interacting with native people.

Charles Fletcher Lummis (1859–1928) was one of these early preservationists, a quintessential pathfinder who searched for a common ground between the public and science. He was one of the early adventurers who visited many Indian communities, even living for a time in the village of Isleta, New Mexico. Lummis was also founder of the Sequoya League in California, an organization whose purpose was to protect and aid American Indians, particularly those of Southern California. The Landmarks Club, another of his endeavors, attempted to preserve California's Hispanic heritage by promoting the restoration of the state's missions.

A Harvard graduate, Lummis became city editor of the *Los Angeles Times*; served as a war correspondent during the Apache Wars; documented and recorded, along with his wife, Eva, the Tiwa language of the New Mexico Pueblos; served as the photographer for Adolph Bandolier's Peruvian expedition; assumed the editorship of the magazine *Land of Sunshine*; designed and constructed El Alisal, his home in Los Angeles; and authored numerous books and articles over a twenty-year period. This journalist, adventurer, photographer, writer, and ethnologist—who walked from Chillicothe, Ohio, to Los Angeles between 1884 and 1885—also organized the Southwest Society as a subsidiary of the Archaeological Institute of America. This became the first Western outpost of the American Anthropological Association and formulated the blueprint for what became known in 1907 as the Southwest Museum in Los Angeles.

Charles F. Lummis wearing a classic Navajo-made poncho (457.G.1; *page 54*), manufactured c. 1840. *Photographer unknown*.

The Southwest Museum: Its Collectors and the Development of a Collecting Aesthetic

When Lummis founded the Southwest Museum ninety-one years ago, his contribution of thirty-four Navajo and Pueblo loom-woven textiles provided the foundation for what would become one of this country's most valuable resources for the study of early Southwestern textile art and history. Among these, three Navajo-made ponchos, four early Classic-style sarapes, two Late Classic-style small blankets, and the early Pueblo blankets and mantas, dating from c. 1840, are the earliest documented examples known in any major American museum in the country.

Lummis's approach to collecting was subjective

Martin de Valle in 1890 wearing a Moki-style sarape or man's shoulder blanket.
Photograph by Charles Fletcher Lummis.

Navajo Early Classic-Style Poncho (*beeldléí* or *baghaltl'óni***), 1840–60**

183 x 138.5 cm

Donor: Charles Fletcher Lummis; 457.G.2

Analysis: This is a plain, weft-faced tapestry weave with lazy lines and warp lay-ins. It is woven of a one-ply, z-spun native handspun churro wool and two- and three-ply, s-spun (sxs) raveled, worsted wools. The dyes are indigo blue, lac, and cochineal. The green is a combination of indigo and rabbit brush. The opening of this poncho is created by a slit tapestry weave, and it is embroidered with one-ply, z-spun, native handspun churro wool, aniline-dyed in yellow-gold. Embroidery also appears near the side selvage. It is native handspun churro wool with a combined indigo and rabbit brush dye, which produces a green color. The white is churro wool with no dye.

and personal. He never participated in planned museum-sponsored collecting expeditions. Instead he put together an impressive collection that grew out of his exotic encounters and experiences with Navajo and Pueblo people. He "salvaged" textiles he considered to be representative of the "true" Indian of the past.

In contrast to contemporaries such as Frank Hamilton Cushing of the Smithsonian Institution, Stewart Culin of the Brooklyn Museum (and previously of the University of Pennsylvania Museum), and George Dorsey of the Field Columbian Museum of Chicago, who amassed collections for preexisting institutions, Lummis dreamed of a future institution to house his collections. The textiles he acquired are wed, in part, to his written accounts in a series of diaries, dating from 1881 to 1882 and from 1888 to 1928, and a corpus of more than thirty boxes of correspondence. Diary entries, written in his "Lummisian" Spanish (Spanish and pidgin English), tell of his encounters with Indians, his purchases, and even what he ate for breakfast, lunch, and dinner. From these, we learn that he bought textiles from residents of Isleta Pueblo, including Francisco Abeita. We also learn of his purchases at Zuni, in Albuquerque and Santa Fe, New Mexico, and at Acoma Pueblo (Lummis Diaries, SWM Library Archives, 1889–1925).

Two of the ponchos and one sarape collected in Acoma in 1889 are well documented. All three belonged to Governor Martin de Valle; two were purchased directly from him, and one was collected later from his son. Of two of the pieces, Lummis wrote in 1925:

> A *bayeta* blanket [457.G.2; *page 56*] like that shown in the frontispiece [*Mesa, Canon, and Pueblo*] is worth thousands of dollars, and another [457.G.1; *page 54*] could not be bought at any price. . . . You can easily reckon that the thread in [457.G.1] cost something at six dollars a pound, and the weaving occupied a Navajo woman for more than a year. It is hardly thicker than the cover of this book, and is almost as firm. . .

Common Threads

Navajo Early Classic-Style Blanket-Sarape (*beeldléí*), 1840–60

173 x 127 cm

Donor: Charles Fletcher Lummis; 457.G.5

Analysis: This is a plain, weft-faced tapestry weave with lazy lines. It is woven of one-ply, z-spun, native handspun churro wool and two- and three-ply, S-spun (sxs) raveled worsted wools. The dyes are indigo blue, lac, and cochineal. The white is churro wool with no dye.

I bought my next-best specimen [457.G.2 *page 56*] in 1889, after weeks of diplomacy, from Martin Valle of Acoma. He bought it thirty years earlier from a Navajo war-chief for a lot of ponies and turquoise. He had used it ever since, but it is as brilliant, and apparently as strong, as the day it was finished.

This Bayeta [457.G.1] of the frontispiece, the most extraordinary blanket I have ever seen, I had known and coveted for many years. It is a shade larger, and was the property of the same dear friend, Martin Valle . . . I tried for many years to get it from him, with all the treasures in my possession—and had many things an Indian loves—but he never would sell. That I have it today is due to the unfilial "Americanized" action of his son, who "held it out on him" and buried him in the next best Navajo (itself worth a king's ransom) and later brought this incomparable one to me. It was too late to "restore" it to brave old Martin; and perhaps in my hands it will wrap his memory longer and warmer than it could have done under the sands of that great, strange Campo Santo in the "City of the Sky."

Lummis had described the third blanket-sarape (457.G.5; *page 57*) thirty-four years earlier, in *Some Strange Corners of Our Country* (1891):

A balleta blanket like that shown in the frontispiece is worth two hundred dollars, and not a dozen of them could be bought at any price. It is seventy-three inches long by fifty-six inches wide, and weighs six pounds. You can easily reckon that the thread in it cost something, at six dollars a pound, and the weaving occupied a Navajo woman for many months. It is hardly thicker than the cover of this book, and is almost as firm . . .

George Wharton James (draped in Navajo blanket) with a group of Navajo men, women, and children in front of an unidentified trading post in Arizona, c. 1901. This photograph may have been taken by Los Angeles–based photographer C. C. Pierce, who traveled with James and later became his business partner, buying the rights to much of his early photography, according to James's stepdaughter, Edith E. Farnsworth.

Does this description sound familiar? It is clear that Lummis used the 1891 description of poncho 457.G.5 as a template for his later 1925 characterization of 457.G.2 and 457.G.1. According to his accounts, both 457.G.5 and 457.G.2 are exactly the same size, which in reality is not the case.

These two descriptions, printed in books published thirty-four years apart, bring into focus the problems today's scholars face in establishing an accurate ethnohistory for early collection pieces—and, of course, in judging the credibility of early collectors. In the case of these three pieces, either the publisher made a terrible error and switched the frontispieces, or Lummis simply chose to use same formula to describe three different textiles. One could also surmise that de Valle purchased all three pieces at the same time from the same Navajo and that the story template therefore fit all three.

Lummis's own aesthetic interests provided much of the motivation for his acquisitions, and he had many opinions regarding the aesthetic nature of Navajo and Pueblo textiles. He described the range of quality in Navajo weaving as being very great, noting that there was a "common" blanket, for bedding and rough wear, which he characterized as "a rude thing." A "second grade of blanket" was described as often being made of Germantown yarns, which the Navajo bought in "big skeins at the various stores and trading posts around their reservation." The designs were ingenious, characteristic of the Navajo, with admirably developed lines.

The colors, however, were another matter entirely. Incensed by the commercialism of these garish fabrics, he decried their "abominable combinations of colors," noting that "some weavers use colors which to an unspoiled Indian are actually accursed—like violet, purple, dark brown, etc.—the colors of witchcraft—and such blankets are worthless to collectors." Bemoaning the fact that it was becoming increasingly difficult to get a blanket with "real" Indian hues, he laid blame on the trader and the ignorant buyer. "One reason the German traders are so successful . . . is that they are willing to humor the customer's 'fool notions'" (1891, 204; 1925, 175–77). When Lummis discussed the early sarape colors that he favored, judging from his own collection, his ethnocentric bias shone forth: "It is curious that these savages should have chosen our own 'red, white, and blue' long before we did," he noted, adding that they had been weaving long before the first Europeans ever saw America.

The patterns of the period also came under Lummis's scrutiny. Firm in his convictions about what a native aesthetic should be, he demanded a return to elegant, simple motifs. He abhorred the use of the "swastika" in Navajo designs, insisting that "it never had any place whatever with the American Indian, and is a cheap modern impudence of traders who have it woven in to please ignorant customers" (1925, 176). Lummis clearly was not aware that this was indeed an authentic Navajo symbol, known as "that which revolves" (*tsil no oli*). He also discussed what he called "the morning star," which was no doubt a romantic,

Juanita, wife of Mañuelito, a Navajo war leader, c. 1901.
Photograph by George Wharton James.

Navajo Woman's Two-Piece Dress (*biil*), 1868–75

129.6 x 81.3 cm (both panels)

Weaver: Juanita (wife of Navajo war leader Mañuelito)

Donor: George Wharton James; 421.G.1115

Remarks: James (1914, 118) wrote: "Specimens of this earlier type of woman's dress are very scarce. Only a few are to be found in museums. The only one I was ever able to secure from the Navajos was one that was made and worn for years by the wife of the great warrior chief Mañuelito. As it was the last of its kind, and was very worn and much repaired, she had carefully washed it and put it away amongst her treasures, from whence she drew it forth to show to me. When I expressed my desire to purchase it she refused to let me have it, on account of its dilapidated condition. But as later we became good friends she finally insisted upon my taking it as a gift. During an Indian fiesta held in Los Angeles I loaned this rare dress, with a score or more of other of my blanket treasures, and when I came to make up an accounting of the 'returns' this was missing, and I have never been able to trace it, to my extreme regret." James must have found this textile subsequent to the publication of his book, because it was in his collection at the time of its donation to the museum. In February 1998 Jennifer Denetdale, Juanita's great-great-great-granddaughter, visited the Southwest Museum and provided an extensive account of this very important woman. Juanita, who was known to the Navajo people as 'Asdzáá Tl'ógi (lady weaver), was born c. 1845 and died in 1910. Family elders report she was born of the Zia clan. Recognized for her ability to persuade people through her speeches, she accompanied Mañuelito to Washington, D.C., in 1874 when the Navajo delegation met with President Grant. "That the wives of Navajo headmen had the authority to speak at public gatherings, including negotiations between Americans and Navajos, suggests the high status in which Navajo women were held in their society" (Jennifer Denetdale, correspondence with author, July 1998).

Analysis: This is a plain, weft-faced tapestry weave with lazy lines. It is woven of one-ply, z-spun native handspun churro wool and two- and three-ply, S-spun (sxs) raveled worsted wools. The dyes are indigo blue, lac, and cochineal in three colors of red, ranging from crimson to a deep maroon; the black-brown color is natural wool with no dye.

Navajo Chief-Style Variant Woman's Wearing Blanket (*beeldléí*), 1880–95

121.9 x 152.4 cm

Donor: George Wharton James; 421.G.1102

Remarks: This textile was originally identified by James as "a man-woven Hopi squaw dress, which, however, I purchased from a Navajo" (1914, 43, fig. 35). He adds, "the man who wove it was a dweller in Tewa or Hano, the first village on the eastern mesas of the Hopis." It is uncertain where James acquired his information about the weaver, but the weave technology would indicate that this blanket is Navajo.

Analysis: This is a plain, weft-faced tapestry weave with lazy lines. It is woven of one-ply, z-spun native handspun wool. The dyes are aniline orange, red, and purple (which has faded); the white and brown wools are natural; and the light brown wool is combed and carded white and brown wool with no dye.

unschooled description of the Le Moyne or Vallero star, a motif that has its roots in the European design repertoire.

Lummis had great enthusiasm for the Indian people with whom he interacted and for what he often referred to as "the primitive life," but he was not ready to adopt it permanently. After living in the Pueblo village of Isleta with his wife, he moved further west. California beckoned, and it did not take long for him to become impressed with the potential of its rich heritage. While living in Los Angeles, Lummis became an incurable collector of songs and poems of early California, paintings of the missions, Indian materials, and books. His vitriolic personality, however, generated both disdain and praise, and he also collected a few enemies.

One such individual was George Wharton James (1858–1923), an "insignificant" in the emerging world of the serious collector-scholar, according to Lummis, who was fierce in his determination to make educated ethnologists privileged purveyors of the "true" Native American culture. Competitiveness, egos, and their professional goals and methods kept the two men at odds. So in the early 1930s, when the George Wharton James collection of ninety-four Navajo and Pueblo textiles was added to the rich assembly of textile material in the Southwest Museum, it also added another layer to our understanding of the complex behaviors and sometimes unorthodox methods of early collectors.

James, like Lummis, espoused a strong sense of social and religious consciousness, particularly with regard to American policy toward the Indian. Like many of his contemporaries, however, James found it

Navajo Woman's Manta (*beeldléí*), 1885–95

106 x 127 cm

Donor: George Wharton James; 421.G.1102A

Remarks: According to James (1914, 42, fig. 32), he purchased this textile in Laguna Pueblo, New Mexico, "twenty years or more" before the publication of his book in 1914. James hung this manta on the door to his library. Correspondence dated 3 November 1913 on letterhead from the Fairmont Hotel in San Francisco lists a "Laguna Squaw dress" with the price of $175. This textile is almost identical in design and style to another Navajo woven manta in the museum's collection (535.G.787). This second manta was donated thirty years after the publication of James's book. The design is part of the Hubbell "revival" rug study and appears in an oil painting of c. 1905 by H. G. Maratta. The manta is an early prototype of the Hubbell "revival" textile.

Analysis: This is a float, with an even 2/2 (diagonal) and diamond twill tapestry weave with lazy lines. Lazy lines are unusual in float weaves but do appear in some early Navajo-woven mantas. It is woven of one-ply, z-spun, native handspun wool and four-ply, z-spun, S-twist machine-spun woolen and worsted wools. An unusual crimson red fiber (cochineal?) is four- and five-ply, S-spun (sxs) raveled worsted yarn. In addition to this cochineal(?)-dyed yarn, there are two more red colors, which are aniline-dyed. Of these two, the coral has shifted from pink. Indigo blue–dyed yarns and yarns spun from the natural dark brown color of the wool are used to define the pattern.

easier to embrace this cause in the abstract, rather than becoming politically and socially involved with the Indian people themselves. Perhaps this is why Lummis was relentless in his campaign to discredit him. James, an art dealer and popular writer, had attempted to breech the walls of serious scholarship, and by Lummis's standards, he was unworthy.

Lummis accused him of improprieties in his research and writing, and he wasn't alone. Many criticized James's overly dramatic, scripted lectures, noting that they were riddled with excessive, "high sounding" verbiage, which he "foisted upon the reading public" (Scott 1957, 379). Others were quick to point out that James's flamboyant writing style was merely a smoke screen to distract the public from his dubious expertise. Lummis, however, went so far as to accuse him of plagiarism.

We must keep in mind, however, that different standards prevailed during the Victorian age, particularly for "popular" lecturers. These podium profiteers were often very casual about crediting their sources, and they were not required to be recognized authorities or have firsthand experience of their subject. The only requirements seemed to be that they have the ability to hold and capture an audience's attention, have a set of slides, and learn the script that went with them. Lummis clearly took exception to this double standard, and this may have led him to condemn James in a scathing editorial entitled "Untruthful James" in the March 1901 issue of *Land of Sunshine*.

Lummis's accusation was based on "Fire Dance of the Navahoes," an article that James published in the September 1900 issue of *Wide World*, a popular magazine originating in London. The account was written in the first person, as if the events had been witnessed and photographed by James himself. Lummis alleged that this was not the case, claiming that the article was "as impudent a fraud as was ever printed" (Lummis 1901, 215–17). He noted that it contained "at least fifteen unquestionable lies, willful and shameless; nine falsehoods which are lies . . . and it is well understood by Indians and Whites, along some 500 miles of the Southwest, that Mr. James may tell the truth when he cannot well help it."

Lummis argued that James had never seen the ceremony and that he "stole" his account and his photographs directly from Washington Matthews, a well-known turn-of-the-century U.S. Army surgeon and sometime ethnologist and specialist in Navajo culture, particularly the weaving industry. In letters to friends and colleagues Lummis suggested that the entire ethic of all of James's work was in question.

James borrowed openly from Matthews, and the latter's work was the basis for much of what James called his own research in his book *Indian Blankets and Their Makers*. Perhaps it was Lummis's invective that led James to declare in this 1914 publication, "In this, as in all my other books, I have cared less about being thought an *original* writer than of giving all possible information about the subject presented. Hence I have gleaned from every known and available source. As a rule, these sources are stated, but if in any place I have failed to give the fullest possible credit it has been through inadvertence, and I hereby extend my apologies and acknowledgments and freely and fully express my obligations" (James 1914, ix).

But no matter what one may say about James's ethics, he was undaunted in his attempt to amass a large collection of Navajo and Pueblo textiles, both as a serious hobby and as a business. Twenty-nine of the Navajo and Pueblo textiles given to the museum in his memory were illustrated in *Indian Blankets and Their Makers*. They included Pueblo manta-dresses, breechcloths, kilts, belts, sashes and Navajo blankets, woman's mantas, Transitional blanket-rugs, saddle blankets, and general area rugs.

Unfortunately, some of the textiles described in the book as being from "the author's collection" are not in the Southwest Museum today. This may be attributed to James's part-time activities as an American Indian art dealer. A few of the blankets illustrated in his book were either traded or sold after its publication. The train pictorial was sold in 1916 for $250 to H. K. Raymenton (SWM Library Archives, James Correspondence: Raymenton to James, 11 October 1916), who donated it to the San Diego Museum of Man in 1939. Another, credited to Hambleton Noel, an Indian trader on the Navajo reservation at the turn of the century, mysteriously remained in James's collection and was eventually given to the Southwest Museum by his stepdaughter, Edith Farnsworth. The dress, or *biil* (*page 59*), that he credited to Juanita, the widow of Navajo war leader Mañuelito, was apparently found after the book went to press and is also in the museum's collection. Several of the textiles were given incorrect cultural affiliations, and in one case a textile he described as belonging to the Fred Harvey Company was inadvertently switched with one from his own collection.

Ironically, the Acoma woman's manta (James 1914, fig. 33), which is credited to the Fred Harvey Company, wound up in the Southwest Museum's collection through the donation of Anita Baldwin approximately twenty years later. One can only wonder if Baldwin saw the manta featured in the James publication and sought to purchase it from Harvey. It was later published by H. P. Mera in 1943 (pl. XXIII ["uppermost panel"]).

Despite its factual errors and "borrowed" research, *Indian Blankets and Their Makers* served a dual purpose, as evidenced by James's subsequent correspondence. It offered him the unwarranted status of "authority," and it promoted his Indian art business. James was a renegade amid the reserved Victorian milieu of his day, an incongruous character of his own design. Though held in contempt, he was never outwardly contemptuous of his peers and contemporaries, including Charles Lummis. He led a frenetic and somewhat eccentric lifestyle but espoused the merits of "calm to a more peaceful life, quiet to deeper enjoyment." His work commingled crass commercialism and self-promotion with very little original scholarship, and despite his championship of American Indian causes, it reflected an ethnocentric and egocentric perspective that was in perfect sync with the times. One moment James would offer elaborate praise of Indian art forms (the very commodity he used to subsidize his lifestyle), the next, he would temper this praise with commentary that proclaimed his innate prejudice: "Yet the Indian—the Navaho, as well as all others—as an Indian, is rapidly disappearing from the land. He is

Acoma Embroidered Brown Wool Manta-Dress, 1860–75

117 x 137.3 cm

Donor: Anita M. Baldwin; 609.G.36

Remarks: This manta was originally attributed to the Fred Harvey Collection, Albuquerque, New Mexico, by George Wharton James, who described it as "ornate and beautiful" (1914, fig. 33, 42). Anita Baldwin must have purchased it from Harvey subsequent to the publication of James's work. In 1943 H. P. Mera published the embroidered panels of this textile in Pueblo Embroidery (pl. XXIII [the "uppermost" band]). In 1989 the textile was reported "missing" from the Southwest Museum collection but was subsequently located and returned to the museum.

Analysis: This is a float diagonal twill weave. It is woven of brown-black one-ply, z-spun, native handspun wool. It was probably woven by a Zuni or Hopi weaver and then embroidered at Acoma Pueblo with three-ply, z-spun, S-twist machine-spun saxony-type red worsted wool and two-ply, z-spun, S-twist native handspun red and yellow-dyed wool. The dyes are cochineal and rabbit brush(?) for embroidery yarns. The dress is natural brown-black wool with no dye. The attached pom-pom tassels on all four corners are of z-spun raveled worsted wool, dyed with cochineal.

slowly changing; not into a civilized being comparable with ourselves, but into a peculiar nondescript, in whose life aboriginal superstitions linger side by side with white men's follies" (James 1914, viii–ix).

The collections and writings of Lummis, James, and other acquisitive adventurers tend, by their very nature, to reveal more about the ideas and tastes of the collectors than they do about the meaning of these objects for the Navajo and Pueblo weavers who created them. These collections were subjective assemblages put together by individuals who thought they knew the true value and meaning of Indian art. In most cases, their writings were anecdotal, and they generally went out of their way to ignore the weavers and their cultures altogether. Though this deficiency can be attributed in part to the language barrier, we cannot dismiss the role played by the attitudes and thinking of the era.

Nevertheless, Lummis, James, and others must be recognized for the contributions to the collections of the Southwest Museum, which continued to grow in the 1920s and 1930s, eventually forming a decade-by-decade record of the Navajo and Pueblo weaving industries. Despite the lack of a "native voice" in the interpretive data that accompanied them, the objects alone became a valuable and fertile resource for later studies.

Navajo Late Classic Small Blanket (*beeldléí*), 1865–85

127 x 82 cm

Donor: Fred Kimpton Hinchman; 535.G.739

Remarks: This textile originally belonged Mark W. Harrington, the father of Southwest Museum curator Mark Raymond Harrington, who purportedly collected it in Mexico in the 1870s. It was purchased from Harrington by Hinchman and appears in Amsden's Navaho Weaving: Its Technic and History *(1934, pl. 68). It is described as a Manchester bayeta. C. N. Cotton purchased this "bayeta" material directly from the Speigelberg brothers of Albuquerque, New Mexico. In July of 1885 he purchased 100 pounds of scarlet red yarn and 20 pounds of dark green. Cotton also purchased limited amounts of white and dark blue. Amsden wrote: "The direct importation of English baize was practiced for years, some dealers calling this category of bayeta 'Manchester' or 'Huddersfield' from the place of manufacture" (1934, 143–44).*

Analysis: This is a plain, weft-faced tapestry weave with lazy lines. It is woven of one-ply, z-spun native handspun wool; one-ply, z-spun raveled worsted wool; and three-ply, z-spun, S-twist machine-spun woolen yarn. The dyes are indigo blue and two greens, one of which combines rabbit brush and indigo and the other of which is aniline. The remaining dyes are of unknown origin.

Navajo Banded Blanket (*beeldléí*), 1880–95

180.3 x 132 cm

Donor: Mrs. Walter Selden Ray; 171.L.5

Remarks: This textile is illustrated in Charles A. Amsden's Navaho Weaving: Its Technic and History *(1934, pl. 34). He wrote: "The orange color probably is an example of the boiled canaigre root, . . . the yellow for a rabbit brush dye, the black made after the formula given for that color. Of the red I am less confident; it may be native, or partly native, but on the contrary may be a faded aniline. All colors but the black are pale and somewhat uneven in tone, a criterion of native dyes."*

Analysis: This textile is a diyugi *plain, weft-faced weave with lazy lines. It is woven of one-ply, z-spun native handspun merino wool. The dyes include indigo and aniline-dyed yarns whose colors have both shifted and faded.*

Charles Avery Amsden (1899–1941), curator-secretary-treasurer of the Southwest Museum, published one of the first creditable studies on Navajo weaving in 1934. Blankets and rugs now in the museum's collection served as the foundation for much of the analytical research published in his now-classic volume, *Navaho Weaving: Its Technic and History*. Many of the textiles illustrated in his study, dating from c. 1800 to 1933, were on loan to the museum at the time of publication and later became gifts.

Amsden's interest in the Southwest and, in particular, Southwestern textiles probably began when he was a young boy and his family moved from Ohio to Farmington, New Mexico. As a budding archaeologist in 1915–17, he was a camp helper on an expedition sent to northeastern Arizona by the Harvard Peabody Museum. As a student at Harvard, he had worked under the guidance of one of America's most renowned Southwestern archaeologists, Alfred Vincent Kidder. Amsden assisted Kidder in his excavation of Pecos, New Mexico. In 1938 he was assigned as archaeologist to the Rainbow Bridge–Monument Valley Expedition of the National Park Service in Arizona, and in 1939 he assisted in excavating the ancient Hopi village of Awatovi on Antelope Mesa in Arizona. This expedition was also funded by the Harvard Peabody Museum. Such work eventually led him to the discovery of early weaving examples in Canyon de Chelly, Arizona, and provided the groundwork for the systematic collecting and research patterns he later developed.

Unlike many of his predecessors, Amsden does not seem to have been a competitive collector. Rather, he collected materials that he liked, that filled gaps in his study, or that were products of dye and fiber experimentation by weavers and traders during the 1920s and 1930s. Many of these became part of the museum's collection; several others were later sold at

COMMON THREADS

Charles Avery Amsden, secretary-treasurer-curator of the Southwest Museum from 1927 to 1940 and author of *Navaho Weaving: Its Technic and History* (1934).

Navajo Chinle-Style Rug (*beeldléí*), c. 1927–28

223.5 x 161.3 cm

Donor: General Charles McCormack Reeve Fund; 491.G.1084

Remarks: This is what is characterized as a Revival-style rug. Cozy McSparron, Sam Garcia, and Mary Cabot Wheelwright encouraged the return to softer vegetal dyes and older patterns in the early "Chinle Revival" style of Navajo weaving. Charles A. Amsden purchased this rug from C. N. Cotton in 1927 or 1928.

Analysis: This is a plain, weft-faced weave with lazy lines. It is woven of one-ply, z-spun native handspun wool. Amsden noted: "The brown [yellow-ocher] is sage or sumac bark dye. The black is a traditional Navajo formula."

Navajo Banded Blanket (*beeldléí*), c. 1933–34

208.2 x 147.3 cm

Donor: General Charles McCormack Reeve Fund; 491.G.1082

Remarks: Charles A. Amsden purchased this blanket from T. D. Seymour, Cozy McSparron's partner, at the Gallup Intertribal Ceremonial in New Mexico in 1933 or 1934. Amsden was interested in the red dyes produced by D. I. Dupont de Nemours and Co. During the 1920s and 1930s McSparron, Seymour, and Sam Garcia had weavers near their trading posts experiment with these commercial dyes. They proved costly, however, and because of the chemical mixing that was required, they were too cumbersome for the Navajo weavers, who had little access to water and other dye supplies.

Analysis: This is a plain, weft-faced weave with no lazy lines. It is woven of one-ply, z-spun native handspun wool. The aniline-derived Dupont red is the only dye in the blanket.

auction in 1992, after the death of his wife, Madeleine.

Unfortunately, only a few of Amsden's field notes, part of the original manuscript of *Navaho Weaving*, an early marked copy of the book, and some correspondence are in the museum's archives today. Thus, what we know of his research techniques and collecting patterns is gleaned from his book and other published monographs, the archival data, and his notes on the textiles he examined. He approached the material "not from the aesthetic, but rather from the technical point of view," Frederick Webb Hodge wrote in the foreword to *Navaho Weaving*. This was clearly the case.

Amsden's book was one of the first to address fiber and dye analysis and to provide a comprehensive review of the technology of the Navajo weaving industry. He actively sought textile examples that would assist him in either confirming or refuting previously published theories about the fibers, dyes, and weaving styles of Navajo blankets and rugs. He began his investigation with a review of the existing literature on the subject, garnering bits and pieces of early Navajo weaving history from earlier writers to add to his own research. His archaeological training aided him immensely.

Amsden examined excavated fabrics as well as contemporary examples, and from these he derived a comprehensive picture of the technology and history. This work—along with Spanish and Mexican historical documents and the renderings of Lansing Bloom, Josiah Gregg, U. S. Hollister, George Wharton James, Washington Matthews (his book is dedicated to Matthews's memory), and John Wesley Powell—aided in his accumulation of an ethnographic record that established the foundation for what became one of the most comprehensive studies ever conducted on the subject. *Navaho Weaving* was in preparation for more than four years.

As was typical, however, of the fledgling anthropological field in which Amsden operated, he tended to regard his predecessors and the objects themselves as his primary informants. He apparently dismissed the Navajo weavers as a source of historical and technical knowledge. Instead he studied private and public collections. He also visited known weaving areas on or near the Navajo reservation during the late 1920s and early 1930s for investigative purposes and met with active Indian art traders.

To add to his own understanding and to enhance the museum's inventory, in 1927 or 1928 Amsden purchased a Revival-style rug from C. N. Cotton in Gallup, New Mexico *(page 65)*. In 1932 he purchased from Cozy McSparron in Chinle, Arizona, an additional Revival-style rug incorporating natural rabbit brush dye. In 1933 or 1934 he attended the Gallup Intertribal Ceremonial and purchased from T. D. Seymour (McSparron's partner) a banded rug incorporating the red color manufactured by D. I. Dupont de Nemours *(page 65)*. Another fascinating rug that apparently was commissioned by Bruce M. Barnard of Shiprock, New Mexico, was made of wools ordered from the Pendleton Woolen Mills in the early 1930s. Barnard created the design, which incorporates several examples of the Vallero star. The weaver is unidentified. Approximately twenty textiles currently in the museum's collection were either purchased by or were at one time in the personal collection of Amsden. Many more received the benefit of his expertise.

The collecting patterns of Lummis, James, Amsden, and other early contributors to the Southwest Museum's textile collection are intriguing, exemplifying the attitudes and assumptions of the decades in which each operated. In the 1930s Amsden laid the groundwork for serious textile scholarship at the museum. The collections and writings of his predecessors reflect the heyday of c. 1900. Lummis and James searched out materials for personal purposes and purchased them whether they were found in an Indian's house, a curio shop, a reservation trading post, or in the hands of others who had interacted directly with Indians. Often little was known about these textiles. Thus, the collector also became the assessor, recording his own subjective judgments in diaries, journals, and correspondence. These, in turn, were transferred to the public record when the collections and archives were donated to the museum.

This type of public record is both the bane and salvation of early textile documentation at the Southwest Museum. We know how and sometimes where the textiles were acquired, but we know little about the makers or about the roles these objects played in the complex social, religious, and economic systems from which they originated.

Fortunately we have developed new approaches. Native artists are becoming primary consultants for museum programming. Textiles and other objects are valued not only for their intrinsic beauty but also for what they can tell us about the people who made them. Moreover, museum patrons are coming to understand that these objects represent a form of collaboration between the artist, the collector, and the museum. Whether this collaboration tells us everything we want to know, or everything we think we should know, may be unimportant as long as the museum remains fertile ground for testing, exploring, and uncovering new opportunities for learning.

It remains an unfortunate circumstance, however, that we know so little about the makers of these early blankets, rugs, and garments because it would be an honor to recognize their individual efforts. We are nonetheless grateful to acknowledge their artistry and to have the opportunity to learn from their work, for these tapestries share the common threads of individual and cultural achievement.

GLOSSARY

balanced: Refers to a fabric in which the warps and wefts are equal in size, spacing, and count.

batting: A type of loosely twisted cotton product; *see also* **roving.**

bayeta: In Navajo weaving literature, fibers from trade cloth that has been raveled, which are rewoven into textiles. Derived from the Spanish word for "baize," this often-misused term has been applied to various types of imported cloth. The earliest of these fibers were raveled from thin, worsted cloth, such as imported English baize, and predyed either with lac or cochineal. Wheat (1981) notes that "woolen" bayeta material was being produced in New Mexico by 1812 but does not specifically designate English baize. Bayeta also refers to American-made flannel and woolen cloths manufactured after the War of 1812, in use on Navajo looms until c. 1885. Bayeta cloth was the primary source of the crimson red color in early Navajo textiles.

carpet yarn: A stiff, rough, coarse, machine-spun yarn with a synthetic dye. It has been observed in Navajo weaving as having from one to three plies.

chief blanket: A commercial term for a Navajo style of men's woven shoulder blanket that was highly favored by the chiefs of many Plains Indian tribes, who bought the blankets for their wives. Its proportions, wider than long, come from ancient Pueblo women's shawls. It is identified by four phases of design development but has a primary background of brown and white alternating stripes.

child's blanket: *See* **small blanket.**

churro sheep: A breed brought to the Western Hemisphere by the Spanish. Its wool is long and silky, with a nearly straight texture and little grease or lanolin. Colors range from black-brown to a creamy white.

Classic period: This term, borrowed from American archaeology of the Southwest, has been used to describe a period in which Pueblo and Navajo weavers were believed to be at the peak of their craft.

    Early Classic: Refers to the period before 1865, a time when finely woven ponchos, sarapes, mantas, and *biils* with simple terraced designs were being produced. During this period European imported materials were generally combined with indigenous fibers, including native handspun wools and raveled cloths dyed primarily with indigo, lac, and cochineal.

    Late Classic: The period from 1865 to 1875, which overlaps with what is known as the **Transitional period**. During this time prespun yarns, cloths, and dyes produced by commercial American manufacturers were being incorporated into Navajo textiles. Outside influences are evident in the designs of all types of woven textiles.

cochineal: A crimson red-purple dye that is extracted from the bodies of small scale insects, generally the female cochineal insect. The Navajo and Pueblo are not known to have used this dye on their own native handspun yarns. Its presence in their textiles comes from raveled predyed commercial cloths.

color shift: A change in the color of dyed yarn due to light exposure (i.e., dark blue shifting to green).

design structure: Basic structural lines used to subdivide a textile's surface area.

diagonal twill: *See* **twill weave.**

diamond twill: *See* **twill weave.**

embroidery: The decoration of a fabric by inserting yarns with a needle. Introduced to the Southwest by the Spanish, embroidery is found in many Classic period and modern Pueblo textiles and occasionally in Navajo textiles.

fiber: A fine thread of cotton, wool, animal hair, bast, or other plant tissue.

float: "Any portion of a warp or weft yarn or supplementary warp or weft yarn that is not interworked with the opposite set but is allowed to run free for a distance on the surface or reverse side of the fabric" (Kent 1983b, 296).

float weave: "[Fabric] on which a pattern is built by warp or weft floats or supplementary warp or weft floats. The term includes twills and weft-float and warp-float pattern weaves" (Kent 1983b, 296).

fugitive color: A dye color that has completely faded to white.

Germantown yarns: The three- and four-ply worsted and woolen spun yarns manufactured in Germantown, Pennsylvania. Three-ply Germantown yarns were introduced into Navajo and Pueblo weaving c. 1864, followed by four-ply yarns c. 1870. Over the decades the term Germantown has come to be used to characterize any fabric with three- or four-ply machine-spun yarns, even those produced by other Eastern mills.

"hills and vales": In Pueblo weaving, the horizontal ridges created by alternating several row groups of uneven twill (e.g., six rows woven over one, under two, followed by six rows of over two, under one).

lac: A resinous substance produced by a scale insect, *Tachardia lacca*, related to the **cochineal** insect. Lac has been used as a dye in India for many centuries. Navajo and Pueblo weavers raveled cloths dyed with lac and rewove the fibers into their own textiles. The earliest lac-dyed yarns are found in Navajo textiles dating to 1750. By 1860 lac was almost completely supplanted by cochineal.

Late Classic. *See* **Classic period.**

lazy line: A diagonal break in the weave of a fabric where a weaver has worked on adjacent areas of a weave. Found in most Navajo and some Zuni textiles, lazy lines allow a weaver to work on a single section of a fabric without having to reach from side to side with each pass of the weft. Lazy lines are generally not used by Hopi or Hispanic weavers.

loom: A frame on which warp threads are attached. The warps are controlled by a loom shed rod and one or more heddles, which are devices that manipulate the warp and help to create the weave. The Navajo and Pueblo use vertical (upright) and backstrap looms.

manta: In the Spanish language, a term for blanket. The term is used to designate wider-than-long cotton or wool fabrics woven by the Pueblo and Navajo and often associated with women's dresses and shawls. Some writers use the term interchangeably with blanket-dress. Mantas are woven in both twill and plain weaves. In an early period they served as clothing for both sexes. Among the Pueblo, Kent (1983b, 55) identifies six types of men's and women's mantas: plaid; white; embroidered white; white with blue, blue and red, or blue and black borders; black; black with blue embroidery.

merino sheep: A European breed issued to the Navajo in the late 1860s, during and after their internment at Bosque Redondo. The wool is crimped, greasy, nubby, and difficult to card and dye.

Moki: In Navajo, Zuni, and Hopi textiles, a simple or complex design of alternating blue and brown stripes. In its simplest form the stripes make up the entire design field. More complex variants feature larger, bolder patterns superimposed over this simple design field. According to Wheat (1976, 427), this style is also called "Mexican pelt" by the Navajo; this is also noted in the *Navajo Ethnologic Dictionary* (Franciscan Fathers 1910). The word was also used by the early Spanish to identify the Hopi Indians. Also spelled *moqui.*

negative design: In Pueblo embroidery, narrow lines of background fabric allowed to show between the embroidered elements of a pattern. This technique has its origins in prehistoric Pueblo design.

plain weave: "A weave in which single weft yarns interlace over and under single warp yarns. When done on a loom, two controls are used—a heddle and a shed" (Kent 1983b, 287). Types of plain weaves include **tapestry, balanced, warp-faced,** and **weft-faced** weaves.

ply: A single strand of yarn or thread; used as a verb, it means to twist several single strands into one. Thus, a three-ply yarn consists of three single-ply yarns twisted together.

raveled: Refers to a yarn that has been produced by disjoining or splitting single- and multi-ply fibers. Single fibers from a woven fabric are taken apart to create individual fine threads. These raveled fibers are utilized in the weaving process as weft threads and are either re-plied or laid side by side (indicated in the analysis as "sxs").

> **early raveled cloth (1750–1865):** A fine cloth commonly dyed with lac or cochineal. The threads were approximately .35 mm. Both Z-spun and S-spun yarns were used until 1825, after which S-spun dominated until 1865. The first cloth raveled by the Navajo and Pueblo was imported through Mexico. (By 1826 it was carried over the Santa Fe Trail and may have been American in origin.) Threads were laid parallel to each other in strands of two to four and then woven into Navajo and Pueblo textiles. Some of the raveled materials in the Massacre Cave fragments may be from *alepin,* a Turkish-Syrian cloth imported into the Southwest via Mexico, or possibly from *cubica,* a comparable Spanish fabric.

> **late raveled cloth (1865–90):** A fuzzy, soft cloth usually dyed with synthetic dyes, though sometimes dyed with **cochineal.** The threads range in diameter from .30 to 1.10 mm, with most either .50 or .90 mm, and are grouped in from two to nine strands. The coarser yarns, used primarily by the Navajos, were gathered from cloth termed **bayeta,** which was supplied to them by the U.S. Army. It was also used in Pueblo textiles. The cloth was no doubt produced in many woolen mills in the East. Also known as *American flannel* and sometimes as *strouding.*

> **raveled machine-knitted yarn:** Identifiable by their very crimped nature, these fibers are usually Z-spun and vary in millimeter size from the late raveled cloth fibers. They can also be worsted or woolen. Although rare, raveled machine-knitted yarn has been observed in post-1875 Navajo blankets.

> **Revival raveled cloth (1885–1900):** A low-quality, aniline-dyed, plain-weave cloth that resembles American flannel. Yarns are approximately .55 mm in diameter. It was supplied to weavers by Hubbell and other traders and used in textiles that copied early Navajo designs. This raveled material is most often observed in the dresses, or *biils,* that Hubbell revived c. 1890.

> **respun and recarded (1865–80):** Fibers raveled from red cloth carded together with white native wool to produce a pink yarn.

> **cloth strips (1870–80):** Cut strips from cloths that did not ravel cleanly.

Revival style: By the twentieth century many of the Indian traders were encouraging Navajo weavers to re-create older blanket patterns and to use natural or vegetal dyes. Juan Lorenzo Hubbell commissioned five artists, including E. A. Burbank, to make paintings of more than one hundred old designs that could be used as templates. Rugs produced from these paintings became known as Hubbell Revivals. In the 1930s Cozy McSparron, Sam Garcia, and Mary Cabot Wheelright encouraged weavers to experiment with softer dye colors. These rugs became known as Chinle Revivals.

roving: An intermediate product of machine spinning. In this process short fibers are discarded, and the remaining longer fibers are combed, carded, and prepared for spinning. The wool is then loosely twisted into a single-ply yarn that appears to be native handspun.

saddle blanket: A textile specifically woven for equestrian use, under the saddle as a saddle pad or over the saddle for comfort and show. There are two styles: double and single. In the literature the early double styles are often confused with "child's blankets." Saddle blankets are usually thick and are often twill woven (although many early double-style examples are weft-faced). Later double-style examples are often distinguished by two distinct patterns. *See also* **small blanket.**

saddle cover: Small, brightly hued textiles, usually embellished with fringe and sometimes with pom-poms. Slightly smaller than a single saddle blanket, saddle covers are often draped over the saddle's pommel as decoration.

sarape: A Spanish term identifying a longer-than-wide "fancy" blanket worn by the Spanish as an outer garment. Also applied to Navajo and a few Pueblo blankets that took on the longer-than-wide trait of the Saltillo-style blanket popularized by the rich Spanish *vaqueros* and *hacienddados* of the seventeenth and eighteenth centuries. Often used interchangeably with the term **shoulder blanket.** Also spelled *zarape* and *serape.*

saxony yarn: An imported fine, three-ply yarn with a high sheen, spun from merino wool, found in Navajo textiles from about 1840 to 1865. Though originally made in Saxony, a former German state, these yarns were later produced in England, France, and New England as well. They were imported across the Santa Fe Trail after 1821. Saxony yarn was dyed with commercial natural dyes of the period (i.e., cochineal and indigo). According to Dooley (1924, 54), all saxony spun yarns are worsted.

selvage: A finished edge of a woven fabric which has been reinforced in some manner to prevent raveling or to strengthen it. In Navajo and Pueblo weaving, in which the textile typically has four complete selvages (two warp selvages and two weft selvages), the selvage is produced by having the weft loop around the side warps and reenter the fabric to weave in the reverse direction and by having the uncut warps loop around the end wefts (Hedlund 1990, 87).

"short rows": A weaving anomaly found primarily in Hopi woven white cotton kilts and mantas, "short rows" are extra wefts that are added within a fabric, often close to the edges. They do not extend back and forth across the length of the textile, but rather in short rows within a certain area. Weavers employ this technique to build up woven rows to maintain an even, flat surface.

shoulder blanket: Blankets characterized by their wider-than-long shape. In early times Pueblos developed several styles. Kent (1983b, 50) suggests that each Pueblo may have had its own style. The Zuni wore very large, coarse plain-weave black wool blankets. Isleta men are said to have had thin, solid blue blankets, also used as burial shrouds. Hopi had the plaid "bachelor's blanket." The Navajo version is the so-called chief blanket.

slit tapestry: A textile in which the weft turns back around the marginal warp of its own area, eliminating a structural connection in the weave (Emery 1980, 79) and producing an open area or slit. This is how the Navajo-made poncho is constructed. Occasionally weavers used this technique to create a small slit in a blanket, which has been called a **spider hole.** *Kilim* is sometimes used as a synonym for slit tapestry.

small blanket: A small woven fabric (usually 125 x 80 cm, but the size can vary). In this text, the term is used as a substitute for the often misleading description "child's blanket." Historical photographs indicate that blankets of this size had multiple uses (as covers for doorways, beds, etc.). Fancy examples of the Classic and Late Classic periods may have also been used as saddle covers.

spider hole: A small, woven-in slit occasionally seen in blankets woven between 1850 and 1900. The term, which may have been introduced by early reservation traders, refers to Spider Woman, the mythological culture hero who taught the Navajo to weave. The cultural meaning of the spider hole may be similar to that of the so-called **spirit line**, or Weaver's Pathway.

spirit line: A small, thin line that extends from a position in the design field to the outside edge of a rug. These lines are frequently placed near a corner of a rug. It is thought that they allow the beauty and energy woven into one textile to be released into the next one made. Also called the *Weaver's Pathway.*

s-spun yarn: Yarn produced by holding a length of fibers vertically and twisting them clockwise, to the right, so that they conform to the center portion of the letter *S*. The use of the lowercase *s* indicates that it is a single ply; the capital *S* indicates the final direction of a multi-ply yarn.

Sunday saddle blanket: A colorful, often highly embellished single- or double-style **saddle blanket**, usually woven in four-ply machine-spun, aniline-dyed yarns with an "eyedazzler" pattern. These are not used under the saddle but are draped over the saddle's pommel and are for show or parade.

sxs: *See* **raveled**.

tapestry: The term generally refers to very finely woven textiles that are believed have been used as wall hangings or decorative fabrics rather than as blankets or rugs. Those made of Germantown or four-ply commercial yarns are also called tapestries.

tapestry weave: Usually a weft-faced plain weave in which the wefts are discontinuous. The term is also used to refer to the technique only when used for pictorial patterning or to very fine mosaiclike patterning with discontinuous wefts. *See also* **tapestry**.

Transitional period: The period from 1880 to 1910, when rapid changes in the social environment were occurring and the Navajo and Pueblo people went from living in a relatively unrestricted geographical area to the reservation setting. At this time new materials and new cultural ideas were introduced, and an increasing number of goods were manufactured for non-Indian use. Textile shapes and textures changed to satisfy new uses and demands.

twill weave: Any of several different types of **float weaves**, all characterized by diagonal alignment of floats for which a minimum of three warp-control (heddles and sheds) groupings is essential.

   balanced twill: A twill in which the weft passes over and under an equal number of warps (e.g., over two, under two).

   unbalanced twill: A twill in which the weft passes over and under an unequal number of warps (e.g., over two, under three).

   diamond twill: A twill whose warp is controlled by the weaver to create weft floats that move both left and right and then reverse to form diamond patterns on the fabric.

warp: Parallel threads and yarns that run vertically in a loom or fabric, crossed at more or less right angles by, and interworked with, transverse **weft** elements. In four-selvage fabrics the long dimension is not necessarily in the warp direction.

warp inserts: Elongated, circular threads that are laid in between original loom warps separated by too much space. There are two types: those laid into the central body of the fabric and those that are laid in and extend to the selvage ends of the fabric. A warp insert is most observable at its beginning and ending junctures, when it appears within the central body of a blanket. Found in Zuni and some Navajo weavings.

wedge weave: An eccentric weave type, found in blankets dating from the 1880s, in which the wefts are placed at oblique, rather than right, angles to the warp to form a series of diagonal, zigzag, or diamond patterns. The warps are pulled from their normal vertical position and, when removed from the loom, form scalloped edges. Also called *pulled-warp weave.*

weft: The transverse elements in a fabric (generally parallel to each other and to the ends of the fabric), which cross and interwork with the **warp** elements at more or less right angles.

weft-faced: Refers to a fabric in which the wefts are sufficiently numerous and compacted to conceal the warps.

woman's wearing blanket: Among the Navajo, a wider-than-long manta-style fabric, similar in pattern and style to the so-called chief's blanket. Distinguished by a design of alternating narrow gray and brown-black or white and brown-black bands that transverse a horizontal axis. The term was probably originated by early nineteenth-century traders, but in Navajo culture the assignment of any gender- or age-specific use to a textile other than the dress, or *biil,* is incorrect.

woolen yarns: Yarns whose fibers are uneven in length and are carded so that they do not lay parallel to each other. These yarns produce a slightly blurred effect in some fabrics with loose weaves or with large patterns that do not have sharp detail. Fabrics produced with this type of yarn, including some four-ply yarns and raveled American flannels, are softer and fuzzier and have more nap and elasticity than other wools. *See also* **worsted yarns**.

worsted yarns: Long-staple yarns that are combed and carded so that the fibers lay parallel to each other and are quite compact. Fabrics created from worsted fibers reflect design detail well and are often used to delineate small, fine motifs in Navajo blankets. The yarns are well suited to weaving long floats because of their strength and are preferred by weavers because they are harder, smoother, and more lustrous than other wools. Early raveled and some three- and four-ply machine-spun yarns may also be worsted. *See also* **woolen yarns**.

z-spun yarn: Yarn produced by holding a length of fibers vertically and twisting them counterclockwise to the left, so that they conform to the center portion of the letter *Z*. Use of the lowercase *z* indicates that it is a single-ply yarn; the capital *Z* indicates that it is the final twist of a multi-ply yarn.

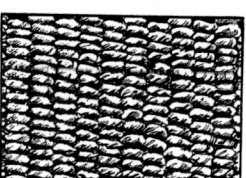

Plain, weft-faced weave

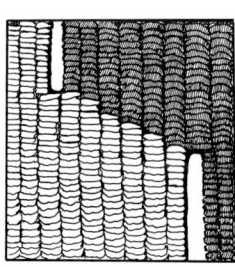

Slit-tapestry weave

Float, diagonal twill weave

A single-ply z-spin

A single-ply s-spin

REFERENCES

Amsden, Charles Avery. 1934. *Navaho Weaving: Its Technic and History*. Santa Ana, Calif.: Fine Arts Press, in cooperation with the Southwest Museum. Reprint, Glorieta, N.M.: Rio Grande Press, 1972.

Bailey, Lynn R. 1964. *The Long Walk: A History of the Navajo Wars, 1846–1868*. Pasadena, Calif.: Socio-Technical Publications.

———. 1970. *Bosque Redondo: An American Concentration Camp*. Pasadena, Calif.: Socio-Technical Publications.

Bancroft, Hubert Howe. 1962. *History of Arizona and New Mexico, 1530–1888*. Albuquerque, N.M.: Horn and Wallace. Facsimile of 1889 edition.

Bent, George. 1841. Correspondence to Manuel Alvarez. Santa Fe, New Mexico State Historical Society, Benjamin Reed Collection. (Microfilm copies in the University of New Mexico Library.)

Cohen, Felix. 1942. *Indian Federal Law*. Albuquerque, N.M.: University of New Mexico Press.

Correll, J. Lee. 1979. *Through White Men's Eyes: A Contribution to Navajo History*. 6 vols. Window Rock, Ariz.: Navajo Heritage Center.

Dooley, William H. 1924. *Textiles*. Boston: D. C. Heath & Co.

Emery, Irene. 1980. *The Primary Structure of Fabrics: An Illustrated Classification*. Washington, D.C.: Textile Museum.

Fane, Diane. 1991. *Objects of Myth and Memory*. Brooklyn: Brooklyn Museum, in cooperation with the University of Washington Press.

Franciscan Fathers. 1910. *An Ethnologic Dictionary of the Navajo Language*. St. Michaels, Ariz.: St. Michael's Press.

Gregg, Josiah. 1844. *Commerce on the Prairies*. New York.

Grinnell, George Bird. 1922. "Bent's Old Fort and Its Builders." *Kansas State Historical Society Collections* 15: 28–88.

Hackett, Charles W. 1937. *Historical Documents Relating to New Mexico, Nueva Vizcaya, and Approaches Thereto, to 1773*. 3 vols. Washington, D.C: Carnegie Institution.

Hafen, LeRoy R., ed. 1930. "The Wm. Boggs Manuscript about Bent's Fort, Kit Carson, the Far West, and Life among the Indians." *Colorado Magazine* (March).

Hedlund, Ann Lane. 1990. *Beyond the Loom: Keys to Understanding Early Southwestern Weaving*. Boulder, Colo.: Johnson Books.

———. 1992. *Reflections of the Weaver's World*. Denver: Denver Art Museum.

Hill, Willard W. 1940. "Some Navaho Culture Changes during Two Centuries" (with a translation of the early eighteenth-century Rabal Manuscript). In *Essays in Historical Anthropology of North America*, 395–415. Smithsonian Miscellaneous Collections, no. 100. Washington, D.C.: Smithsonian Institution.

James, George Wharton. 1914. *Indian Blankets and Their Makers*. Chicago: McClurg & Co.

Kent, Kate Peck. 1957. "The Cultivation and Weaving of Prehistoric Cotton in the Prehistoric Southwestern United States." *Transactions of the American Philosophical Society* (Philadelphia) 47, no. 3.

———. 1983a. *Prehistoric Textiles of the Southwest*. Santa Fe, N.M.: School of American Research.

———. 1983b. *Pueblo Indian Textiles: A Living Tradition*. Santa Fe, N.M.: School of American Research.

Lummis, Charles F. 1891. *Some Strange Corners of Our Country*. New York: Century Company.

———. 1901. "Untruthful James." *Land of Sunshine* 14 (March): 215–17.

———. 1925. *Mesa, Cañon, and Pueblo*. New York: Century Company.

Mera, H. P. 1943. *Pueblo Indian Embroidery*. Memoirs of the Laboratory of Anthropology, no. 4. Santa Fe, N.M.: Laboratory of Anthropology. Reprint, Santa Fe, N.M.: William Gannon Edition, 1975.

Navajo Community College. 1973. *Navajo Stories of the Long Walk Period*. Compiled by Ruth Roessel. Tsaile, Ariz.: Navajo Community College Press.

New Mexico State Law Library. 1869. *United States v. Lucero*. 1 N.M. 442, 438, 442. Santa Fe, N.M.

———. 1913. *United States v. Sandoval*. United States 231. 28:39–41. Santa Fe, N.M.

New Mexico State Record Center, Spanish Archives (NMSRC-SA). 1800. June 21. Chacon to Nava. Document #1492. Santa Fe, N.M.

Scott, E. B. 1957. *The Saga of Lake Tahoe*. Rev. ed. Lake Tahoe, Nev.: Sierra-Tahoe Publishing Co.

Thompson, Gerald. 1976. *The Army and the Navajo: The Bosque Redondo Reservation Experiment, 1863–1868*. Tucson: University of Arizona Press.

Wheat, Joe Ben. 1976. "Documentary Basis for Material Changes in Design Styles in Navajo Blanket Weaving." In *Irene Emery Roundtable on Museum Textiles, 1976, Proceedings: Ethnographic Textiles of the Western Hemisphere*, 420–44. Washington, D.C.: Textile Museum.

———. 1981."Tension and Harmony: The Navajo Rug." *Plateau* 52, no. 4: 2–9.

Whitaker-Bennett, Kathleen. 1981. "Navajo Chief Blanket: A Trade Item among Non-Navajo Groups." *American Indian Art Magazine* 7, no. 1: 62–69.

Wright, Barton. 1979. *Hopi Material Culture*. Flagstaff, Ariz.: Northland Press.

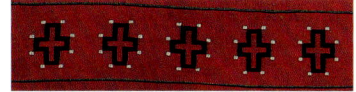

ACKNOWLEDGMENTS

Many individuals have assisted me in organizing this exhibition and the accompanying catalogue. The languages of the Pueblo and Navajo are not written, so in an attempt to avoid adding to the welter of spellings that have been suggested in the past, I solicited advice from a number of specialists. For translations from Hopi, I relied primarily on Hopi linguist LaVerne Masayesva Jeanne of the University of Nevada, Reno. For Navajo translations, I was assisted by Indian trader R. Bruce Burnham of the Navajo reservation at Sanders, Arizona, who also offered invaluable opinions on the museum's Navajo textiles. Young and Morgan's *The Navajo Language: A Grammar and Colloquial Dictionary* (1987) aided in Navajo orthography. Advice on Zuni materials came from Joseph Dishta, Loren Panteah, and their colleagues at the Zuni Cultural Preservation Office. Zuni translations were provided by Vernon Quam of the Zuni Museum. Lee Lomayestewa of the Hopi Cultural Preservation Office reviewed the manuscript and provided additional information. Special thanks are extended to Jennifer Denetdale—a descendant of Juanita, wife of the war leader Mañuelito—who provided invaluable background on her family history.

Many institutions and their professional staffs helped me in gathering data. At the Hubbell Trading Post in Ganado, Arizona, Bill Malone reviewed all the color rug plates and generously shared his knowledge; Maralyn Yazzie provided moral support. The National Park Service, Hubbell Trading Post, under the guidance of Superintendent Nancy Stone and Curator Ed Chamberlin, provided hospitality and access to the Hubbell archives. At the Farmington Museum, Catherine Davis, librarian, and Julie Platt, curator, furnished archival materials and photographs.

This publication benefited from the expertise of many people. In addition to those already mentioned, I called upon Mark Winter, owner of the Toadlena Trading Post on the Navajo reservation, and Nancy J. Blomberg, curator of native arts at the Denver Art Museum. The maps were developed by Apache-Zapotec artist Bernie Granados Jr. The graphics were created by Jack McCord.

Although all major projects tax the resources of the organizing institution, this one, drawn exclusively from the permanent collection, has required an unusual degree of collaboration within the museum. I gratefully acknowledge the Southwest Museum Board of Trustees—particularly Michael Heumann, Caryll S. Mingst, Jim Phillips, and Charmay Allred—and the museum staff. In addition, several individuals have worked daily (including weekends) on a volunteer basis over the past year and a half. These volunteers offered support at all stages of the project, and without them it might still be in progress. Susie Hart was responsible for the textile analysis, helping to identify fibers, dyes, and weaving construction for more than three hundred textiles. Hugh Stevenson worked with me to compile, for the first time in the museum's history, a comprehensive inventory of its Navajo and Pueblo textiles. They were later joined by Ann Marie Donoghue, to whom I owe a great debt for inputting the textile inventory and analyses into a database and tirelessly rechecking for mistakes or omissions. John Donoghue designed the database for this study and provided computer systems support. Jerry Mendelson typed the first draft of the inventory from the ARGUS printout, and Norm Rogers guided us through some of our early computer glitches. Linda L. Quinn, Judy Parker, Mary Oliver, Dane Hart, Patricia Heidelberger, Robert Curry, Phil Skonieczki, and Merlin Carlson generously assisted with organizational and research tasks and with many other facets of the project.

Finally, I would like to dedicate this work to my father, Wesley F. Whitaker, and to my mother, Mildred F. Whitaker, who regretfully did not live to see this study completed. They and my darling daughter, Brooke Dawn Bennett, have been the guiding forces in all that I do both personally and professionally.

K. W.

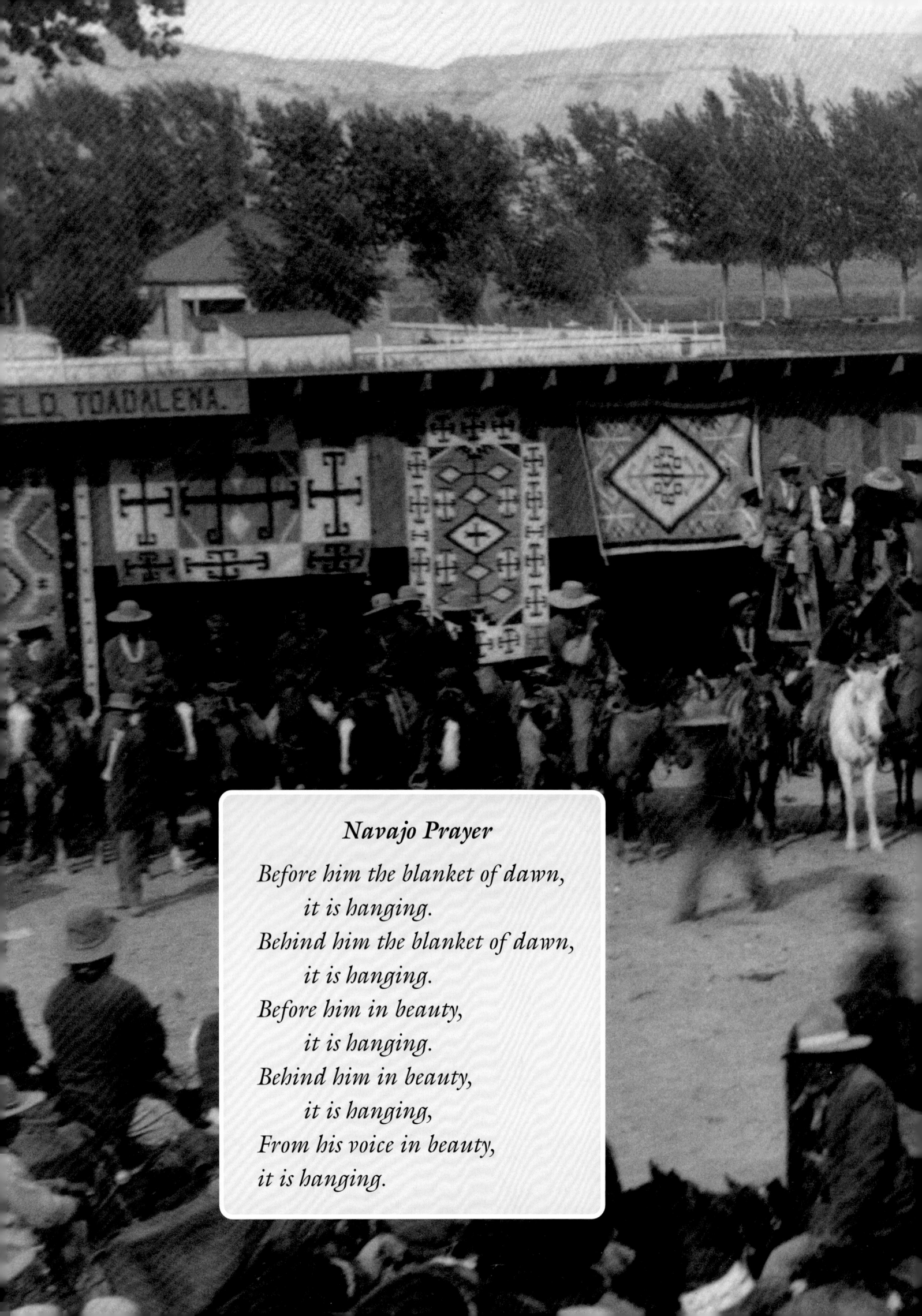

Navajo Prayer

Before him the blanket of dawn,
　it is hanging.
Behind him the blanket of dawn,
　it is hanging.
Before him in beauty,
　it is hanging.
Behind him in beauty,
　it is hanging,
From his voice in beauty,
　it is hanging.